Noe Street Home, San Francisco, 1967 (JIM MARSHALL)

JANIS

Written and Edited

BY

DAVID DALTON

A Stonehill Book

published by

SIMON AND SCHUSTER

NEW YORK

To

A.D., S.D., and K.

with love

Possession is then, the Real Principle of all
that exists, for nothing can bind itself to another without Love, which of all things is the
most willful. Homeless, bedless, and barefooted,
she operates by mere presence, as if Melody herself were plucking the string. . . .

—*Plotinus*

Designed by
GEORGE DELMERICO

FIRST PRINTING

SBN 671–21088–2 Casebound edition
SBN 671–21089–0 Touchstone paperback edition
Library of Congress Catalog Card Number: 72–159128
Manufactured in the United States of America

ACKNOWLEDGMENTS.

I would like to thank all those whose affection, patience, and enticement have encouraged me in the writing of this book. I would like to thank Jonathan Cott for writing the preface and for permitting me to use sections of "The Million Dollar Bash," written jointly for *Rolling Stone,* as the basis of Part Four of this book. To Danny Moses for his patient weeding of overgrown passages. To Jeffrey Steinberg for his energy and personal prestidigitation, and to George Delmerico for his insight and care in the designing of the book.

I would also like to thank Myra Friedman, Eric Andersen, and Chet Flippo for all their help in the many aspects of this book.

I would like to thank Jann Wenner for permitting me to quote freely in the text from all articles by myself and others that appeared in *Rolling Stone* and for allowing me to reprint all major articles pertaining to Janis that appeared in the magazine. In this regard, I would also like to gratefully acknowledge the original writers of those pieces: Stanley Booth, John Cooke, Jonathan Cott, David Felton, Chet Flippo, Ralph Gleason, Tony Glover, Paul Nelson, and Paul Shadoian.

Acknowledgment is gratefully made to the following for permission to quote from copyrighted material: New Directions for the quotations from *The Crack-Up* by F. Scott Fitzgerald, Outerbridge & Dienstfrey for quotations from *They Became What They Beheld* by Edmund Carpenter and from *No One Waved Good-bye,* and Harper & Row for quotations from *Zelda* by Nancy Milford, and from Mircea Eleade's *Myths, Dreams and Mysteries.*

PREFACE.

"IT IS NOT GOOD," Goethe said to Eckermann in one of their first meetings, "that you pass through here so quickly. I would like to see more of you and speak to you more." And he concluded a letter to his future chronicler by writing: "Rejoice with me in the expectation of a prolonged and intimate acquaintance."

"I was happy to be near Goethe again," Eckermann writes, "and I felt myself committed to him with my whole being. If only I have *you* and can have you, I thought, then everything else will be right with me too. And so I told him again that I was ready to do whatever he thought best for me in my particular situation."

"I'm going to write a book about you," David Dalton told Janis Joplin when she was beginning her first tour with her Full Tilt Boogie band in Louisville, Kentucky.

"Honey," Janis replied in partying manner and with an eye to the future, "if you can pay for the plane tickets, then you can follow me around for the rest of my life."

In the beginning of July 1970, David and I were riding the Festival Express, the amazing communal train trip from Toronto to Calgary on which Janis played a funky Eleanor of Aquitaine-Catherine the Great queen to a court of jamming musicians including the Grateful Dead, Delaney and Bonnie, Buddy Guy, Eric Andersen, and Ian and Sylvia.

One afternoon, as the train sped through the Saskatchewan plains, Janis and Bonnie Bramlett were conversing in the bar, having invited David and his cassette machine to record the dialogue, when David's tape ran out. Janis was just beginning to recount her experience of being on stage for the first time with Big Brother and the Holding Company.

"They threw these musicians at me, man, and the sound was coming from behind, the bass was charging me, and I decided then and there, that was it, I never wanted to do anything else. It was better than it had been with any man, you know. Maybe that's the trouble. . . . Hey, where's David?"

"He went to get a tape," I said.

"Goddamn, he's missing great stuff here. Hey, David! Get back on in here!"

The night before we reached Calgary, Janis was dressed up for the journey's most glittering and happiest hours. A "bacchanalian Little Red Riding Hood with her bag full of tequila and lemons, lurching from car to car like some tropical bird with streaming feathers," as David described her, she sat in with about fifteen musicians and sang renditions of "You've Got to Hide Your Love Away" and "Bobby McGee." Finishing a song, she said something and cackled, then turned around to David, asking, "Are you remembering what I just said, honey?" Transported and in deep reverie, David mumbled a complaisant "Sure, Janis"—a Boswell caught thinking of everything but the ineluctable modality of the visible and audible.

But David Dalton remembers everything because he knows how to create the spaces, colors, and garbs in which the protean goddess Mnemosyne reveals herself. He is a writer who not only identifies with his subject in an act of total sympathy but also perceives the mana implicit in the artist's persona. He sees shamanistic and thaumaturgical realities as clearly as Blake's fools saw only guineas in the sun. His "mythy" mind operates at the service not so much of some kind of "explanatory" psychological map but rather of an interconnecting web that illuminates and fosters an enrichment of true personality. The most he can do, in Jung's terms, is "to dream the myth onwards and give it a modern dress." Janis found a biographer whose alchemical art intensifies and transmutes his subject, just as she transformed herself: *To love is to transform and be transformed.*

JONATHAN COTT,
Rolling Stone

CONTENTS.

PART THREE.

THE CATTERPILLER ON THE LEAF

PART FOUR.

ENTRAIN'D SEAS

PART FIVE.

PHOTOGRAPHS

PART SIX.

FUGITIVE PIECES
(*EXCERPTS FROM* ROLLING STONE)

PART SEVEN.
SONGS

A 33 rpm record of
Janis singing and talking
follows page 20.

PART ONE

SOUTHERN TALES

HENRY: I believe that phantasms are nothing
but a little unbalanced condition of our mind:
images that we fail to hold within the boundaries of the kingdom of sleep. They appear
even in the daytime; and they terrify. I am
greatly frightened when at nighttime I see
them before me—disorderly images that,
having dismounted from their horses, laugh.
I am sometimes afraid, even of my blood that
throbs in my veins like the thud of steps resounding in distant rooms in the silence of
the night.
—Pirandello, *Henry IV*

PART ONE

SOUTHERN TALES

Waking Dreams

BELOW THERE IS NOTHING. Only an amorphous white element, fields of white foam that seal us off from the world beneath. The only distraction is the rain pitting the translucent geography of the plane window where minuscule rivers begin and end in the twinkling of an eye.

Janis is reading, swimming off into a firmament of her own, burrowing into the leaves of *Zelda,* its jacket a nest of flamelike peacock feathers that glow with greenish patina in her ringed hands, more like a chunky bouquet than a book.

Janis reads a lot, and these books (*Tender Is the Night, Look Homeward, Angel, The Crack-Up*) that she lugged about with her on her journeys had a curious effect, that almost approached possession, on her subterranean personal life, their words and images, like spores falling on fertile inner tracts, pollinating her daydreams.

Strangely enough, and perhaps fortunately for Janis, all this reading, absorption and general intellectual turn of mind did not intrude on her singing and songwriting, which always remained very basic, gutsy, immediate and devoid of reflection. Her considerable intelligence, in fact, did not prevent her from producing the delicious, brassy and super-corny imagery of some of her songs ("Love Is Like a Carrot" from "Move Over"). She somehow managed to separate the desperately reflective side of her character from her music and her presence on stage. In the quiet hours, however, before going on stage, on planes, in airports and all the vacant moments of life on the road, the tiny roots of sympathy slipped out of the pages and buried themselves in her mind's eye, infusing her waking dreams with the traces of fine summery afternoons or sultry evenings of more than sixty years ago.

Are you digging it?

The book or Zelda? I'm not crazy about the book, man, but her life, man, that is something else. She was fucking crazy as I am. I was just reading about how she was at this dance, and afterwards in her velvet gown and carrying a bouquet of roses—you wouldn't believe how romantic her whole thing is, course it was a very romantic time—anyway she's coming back from this dance and she's passing this photography shop that has a photograph of one of Zelda's beaus in the window. This chick that's with her makes some dumb remark about how he ought to be with her rather than being in the shop window. So you know what she does, man? She kicks in the glass right there and takes out his photograph and walks away bold as brass with it and takes it to this café with her just like she was on a date. I mean she was *real* crazy, you know?

Didn't she flip out in the end?

Yeah, well, that was a lot later. She wrote these heartrending letters to Scott. She was in a lot of institutions. I think everything that happened to her was just too much in the end. What I'm trying to say is that she had all these romantic aspirations and stuff and they all *really* happened to her eventually. So what I think is that that just freaked her out, it's like having a dream about something and then it actually happens.

From letters Zelda wrote from Dr. Forel's clinic:
Dear Scott,
    . . . I want to get well but I can't it seems to me, and if I should whats going to take away the thing in my head that sees so clearly into the past and into dozens of things that I can never forget. Dancing has gone and I'm weak and feeble and I can't understand why I should be the one, amongst all the others, to have to bear all this—for what? . . .
    Yesterday I had some gramophone discs that reminded me of Ellerslie. I wonder why we have never been very happy and why all of this has happened— It was much nicer a long time ago when we had each other and the space about the world was warm—Can't we get it back someway—even by imagining? . . .
                                                                    Zelda

Janis opens *Zelda* to the center where there are photographs of her and Scott, old snapshots and drawings, the comings and goings of a life. Zelda in a ballet costume—ruffles of tulle and ribbon encircle her like a precocious flower. In a little picture entitled "Folly" she is sitting in a field of flowers as if she'd just sprung up. Janis is as familiar with all these hieroglyphs of Zelda's life as she might be of her own. She seems to bounce on and off the pages as if they were little gray mirrors as our eyes walk about the pages. Here's a drawing by Ring Lardner of Zelda that's been glued onto an old newspaper clipping. She is dressed in a winky Petty-girl jazzy coat as she steps onto this unexplained ledge of question marks. On a following page there is a more gloomy image entitled ominously "Recovered." The intense, staring, oscillating

eyes, barely able to contain the madness behind them, glare out of a tensely drawn face framed by a short institutional haircut.

What happened before and after these moments, an afternoon in the middle of a field in 1916? They are enigmatic as photos we now have of Janis. Janis is fascinated by and envious of Zelda at the same time, this wild Southern girl named after a gypsy queen in a sentimental novel by her romantic mother, growing up with the century—the automobile, the airplane, all the supercharged cathexis of the American dream, which, similar to Janis's Zelda are magical chimeras bought with the currency of wishes, half fantasy, half object. Janis glumly points out the last photograph of Zelda in the book. Appropriately she is standing rather stiffly in the bucket of a huge crane as if about to be lifted off the earth. "How our love shone through any old trite phrase in a telegram," Scott wrote in one of his jottings collected in *The Crack-Up*. This sentence is realized in a photograph of Zelda's scrapbook where cables from Scott are pasted like little white clouds with devotional care.

Growing up in the Deep South had a lot to do with the concreteness of Janis's vision of herself—the gin-soaked barroom queen from Memphis—because the South with its ruminant, brittle gentility—like Tennessee Williams' vulnerable romantic women whom Janis also resembled—seems to hoard up time, relatively sheltered as it is from the changes of a more fluid society.

Janis also shared with Zelda the almost literary tenets of Southern womanhood, the spirited veneer of the legendary Southern belle with its attendant charades of etiquette that are still a fact of life in the Deep South. They both grew up in this claustrophobic atmosphere with its elaborate anachronistic modes of proper behavior which unconsciously support a delicious irony: that well-brought-up Southern girls grow up under

similar halters of tradition and confining so-
cial restrictions as the Southern black. It
was, perhaps, this perverse affinity that gave
such credence to Janis's blues.

Both willful, headstrong girls, at the same
time sensitive enough to appreciate the lush
romantic tradition that they grew up with,
Janis and Zelda were torn between wanting
to tear down all the silly pretenses of this
feudal society with its faint echoes of Sir
Walter Scott tiptoeing about Tara and living
gracefully within its many privileges. Such a
conflict had one day driven Zelda to write:
". . . it's very difficult to be two simple
people at once, one who wants to have a law
to itself and another who wants to keep all
the nice old things and be loved and safe and
protected."

*How did you come to get into this strong
identification thing with Zelda?*

I always did have a very heavy attachment
for the whole Fitzgerald thing, that all out,
Full Tilt, Hell Bent Way of Living, and she
and F. Scott Fitzgerald were the epitome of
that whole trip, right? When I was young I
read all of his books; I've reread them all:
autobiographies, *The Crack-Up,* all the little
scribblings . . . and she was always a mythic
person in his life, you also have the feeling
that he destroyed her. You always get the
feeling that she was willing to go with him
through anything and that he ruined her. But
in the book you find out that she was just as
ambitious as he was, and that they sort of
destroyed each other. He wrote her a letter
one time in which he says, "People say we
destroy each other, but I never felt we destroyed each other, I felt we destroyed
ourselves."

Why are you so attracted to them?

Are you trying to find out if I identify with
them?

Yeah.

Yes, of course I do. That's obvious. We've
got sort of the same trip going. But she was
luckier, she had him. She found a part of
herself. But I do not think that the end she
came to is necessarily a product of that. It
seemed to be more because of her thwarted
ambition and her Southern childhood that
dropped her. But I haven't finished the book
yet. Oh my god, she had such a beautiful way
with words. . . . Fitzgerald took a lot of
things from her, lifted things from her diary,
she was every one of his female characters—
Nicole Diver, the charming woman, she was
all of them. She wrote, too, but he would take
her stories and publish them under his own
name. That was their deal. Anything she
wrote or said he got to use it in his work. She
was a very romantic character, and I have a
very high sense of the romantic, as you may
have noticed.

*Yeah, I've noticed a lot of things you are
into are in that 20's and 30's type of thing.*

I'm an anachronism, that's what it is.

How did you get that way?

I don't know, man. I mean I'm not a 1930's
anything, I'm just a 50's chick, but I suppose
my thoughts and fantasies go to that . . .
more expansive, more abandoned time, you
know? Not those coy games people like to
play, not like the little flirt games, you know.
More like, "Well, boys?" Doesn't seem to be
doing me too much good either, but you
know, they'll all come around.

Do you identify with Mae West then?

Oh, yeah, she's dynamite, but, uh, I think I
have too much insecurity . . . reality and
humanness . . . I could never, I mean I may
say it, but I don't mean it. I don't know her
well enough to know whether she means it or
not either. I think she probably even *means*
it. I can pull it off, you know . . . but any-

body that knows me knows . . . But I like that style, I like that way of living, I like that way of looking at things. It's down to gut level, man. The truth, man. It's down. I'm hungry, feed me, make me happy. . . .'' [*In a throaty whisper*] "Come here . . . whoooo!''

Parasites descending out of time fall on the exposed and innocent. They often choose as their victims the naïve, and all those who seem to remember in their wistful eyes a nostalgia for paradise.

Janis was one of these naïve people. Being naïve has nothing to do with how much you know or read, it is expecting things to happen against all the obvious indications, impossible hopes, expecting things will turn out all right in the end.

Zelda, Bessie, Billie and Nicole Diver were her immaterial doubles, cores which Janis reached by intoxicating herself with their lives. Possession induced by fantasies. Janis's flirtation with these departed spirits was a very real traffic with ''let's pretend,'' encouraging all beautiful, silky, seductive shades that try with their fatal suckers to attach themselves to the living.

These ideas of possession, although they appear to be only mental images, come in fact from our bodies, the re-emergence of the self, the true thread. The problem is to find out who you were, to put someone on so they shine through you. Matching codes with cores.

Janis's restlessness came from the static of all these voices, the ceaseless chatter of those who inhabit the possessed and make it impossible for them to live their lives simply. At every moment a host of presences is moving under the surface with its mass of unlived lines.

Perhaps Janis found refuge in this cosmic narcissism that gradually became more real than whatever remained of herself. These disguises seemed to relieve her of the responsibility for her own existence. Crawling into the lives of others she set at rest momentarily the forces within her and without her, triggered as they often were by her own volition, which constantly seemed to seek out her own destruction.

The impersonations (putting on Bessie for the blues) were not simply representations but very *real* identifications. They went beyond and preceded her knowledge. Janis was already living out pieces of Zelda's life before she knew who Zelda was.

These spirits lie in wait in images, words, and songs, waiting for the accidentally left open window to the past that will give access to these temporal vampires. They fly in at the brain and spring forth at the least identification. In daydreams they take possession of us.

And again perhaps all these identifications, impersonations and put-ons of others are not really sinister at all but are no more than correspondences with the slow, monotonous, and imperceptible convolutions of time of which these parasitic images are just manifold effects and manifestations. Is it this that gives rise to those truisms that the recently departed always elicit? Saxophonist Martin Fierro, playing with Quicksilver, on the night Janis died: "She's here tonight, man. You know what I mean? She's in everybody's heart, mouths, and heads. Everybody says, 'I wish she's here.' She's in my heart, man, screaming . . . laughing . . . bitching, man, bitching.''

They are not *really* dead we just lose track of the thread for the moment, because *we* open the doors to these violently egotistical forces latent in every form but most powerfully so in music because songs exist only in the present. Consummations devoutly to be wished. We give them shelter simply by expelling the more trivial aspects of ourselves. The obsession with history, the tailing of exemplary lives is necrophilia, marching in parades of lost souls that revive when we listen to their tales, breath of these bones, the tales of time. Images infest the living everywhere, in songs, words, in old pictures from a remote time: for Janis, the 20's, crystal, intangible, frozen and silent except for the voices that we give them.

It is only a short step from the confusion of things with their attributes to incorporation. In its most real sense and with its double meaning we put Janis on every time we listen.

East of Eden

Americans, he liked to say, should be born with fins, and perhaps they were—perhaps money was a form of fin. In England, property begot a strong place sense, but Americans, restless and with shallow roots, needed fins and wings. There was even a recurrent idea in America about an education that would leave out history and the past, that should be a sort of equipment for aerial adventure, weighed down by none of the stowaways of inheritance or tradition.
—F. Scott Fitzgerald, *The Crack-Up*

JANIS KNEW THAT when people talked about "Janis" they were talking about the mythical Janis, that *Cashbox* called a "kind of mixture of Leadbelly, a steam engine, Calamity Jane, Bessie Smith, an oil derrick and rotgut bourbon, funneled into the 20th century somewhere between El Paso and San Francisco."

It was very easy to pick up on just this side. It was the Janis everybody always talked about—the mind's-eye Janis, gutsy, ballsy, funky—and it was also the easiest Janis to write about. Predictably, it was the only Janis that ever got into print. There was nothing enigmatic or ambivalent about it. Janis barreling into town, trading raunchy stories with the boys, setting up drinks. It

was so "put together." Small-town journalists in the South and Midwest lapped it up, a bit of color in between the announcements. They were just witness to a good performance.

An editor at *Esquire* barks: "I'm tired of Janis Joplin stories, it's always the same damn thing."

Raunchy and hayseed as she came on, Janis was no doggone rube from a high-grass town. She was brought up in cities—Port Arthur, Austin—with all the predictable certainties of middle-class American life, which don't change much from one state to another, bound together as it was then by the insidious cohesions of *Life* magazine, Ozzie and Harriet, Kleenex, Coca-Cola, Perry Como, and the *Saturday Evening Post*. It was an act of will and supreme imagination on Janis's part that sustained the illusion, the *child's dream of space* in which she moved, and that she realized in herself. The amazing thing was that you could actually see the traces of all these places—Kokomo, East Helena, the South Side of Chicago—and all the people she had never known but who had nevertheless grown into her: the whole childhood of America—endless spaces, wagons, frontiers, the iron horse, the restlessness of purpose in the promised land, impossible longings, *aerial adventures*. Janis was an "American value," as Gerald Fitzgerald (Scott's brother) had said of Zelda. And as she said of herself, she was a deliberate, contrived anachronism, an American beauty grown ripe on memories, the romantic, heroic, practical Republican testament of self-help, industrious Eden from the missionary times, the vanished mirage of America. A peaceable, primitive kingdom, a pure elemental vision that still lingers on California citrus labels.

Below, the real landscape has reappeared, the mist drifting away suddenly like a book of colors opened to Kentucky. The stage for the afternoon is being set. Ladies and gentlemen, on your right is the Ohio River, played this afternoon by the letter S. The patches slide by below, yellow, red, brown, as articulately spaced as regional areas in a geography book, where each color knows its order. Flipping the pages of Kentucky, Louisville dramatically appears in due course in the form of the letter T, like a letter dropped from a giant alphabet, extending its arms nine miles along the Ohio River, its tail curling up into the hills.

"I'm Saving the Bass Player for Omaha"

FULL TILT BOOGIE were a strange group in relation to Janis, all of them (except Clark) almost a decade younger than she was, and Janis was inclined to treat them with the maternal solicitousness of an aroused stepmother. It worked out well. They were not as intimate as Big Brother, which resembled a real family with all the turbulence of unconditioned ups and downs that caused very real damage to the equilibrium of the group. On the other hand they did not share the anonymity of the second band with its Motown-like line-up. A very deep, almost tangible affection flowed between Full Tilt and Janis, and it showed in the joy they always generated on stage. It *was* a weird troupe, though: earthy, jaded, outrageous Janis and Full Tilt, who for the most part were quiet, introspective and innocent by comparison.

On tour, only Clark's raucous voice would compete with Janis's in the muffled hum of planes, coming on in his best Dodge City

manner to some rinsed-out blonde with about as much subtlety as a fat-back slam.

But the quiet, inward qualities of Full Tilt were a perfect foil for Janis, and she stood out in brilliant relief against their muted, subtle personalities somewhat like the Midnight Special panting down the track must have stood out against a moonlit night.

Sometimes, like when an R. Crumb special came jiggling her beebite boobies down the aisle, stuffed into a pair of faded jeans, Janis, feeling their reticence insulted the self-respect of red blooded American womanhood would alert "the boys" with a loud "BING—GO!"

The group had a certain dignity about them, emanating in part from John Cooke, maybe the most urbane road manager in all rock. In his cowboy trophies from Miller's Western Outfitters in Denver he looked like the only possible marshal from Cambridge, Massachusetts.

John is reading too (a chronicle of the Kiowa Indians), but his America is further back than Janis's, back "beyond the rolling hills of the Republic," Injuns and army scouts, Lewis and Clark, the tantalizing secrets of the frontier.

Brad is grinning inanely at some interior joke, with that innocent vacant *Hee-Haw* grin. Richard taps his spooky harmonies on a silent piano, and Ken and John Till, wired with earphones to their private universe, trade tapes of Hendricks and Ross, Coltrane, and King Biscuit Boy.

"Basically, we are like studio musicians who were put together for a session," Ken Pearson, the organist, explains with his characteristic modesty. "It's not like we played together in the garage for three years before making it. We are still finding out what kind of music we like. I'll go over to John's room, and he'll play me something and I'll say, 'you mean, you like *that?*' You know, we're just a group of musicians from really different backgrounds, thrown together, slowly becoming a family."

Ken himself worked with a lot of small rock and jazz bands in Canada. He backed up folk singer Ronny Abramson and played with Penny Lang's Montreal Symphony 1500 before joining Jesse Winchester about a year ago as a piano player. Jesse had come north to avoid the draft and had planned to head west with his four-man band in an old bus, just stopping and doing a number wherever they happened to be, when Robbie Robertson offered to record him. Robbie had got together a bass player and a drummer for the session, but still needed a keyboard, so Jesse and Ken were the only members of the original group to play on the album. Ken would probably have stayed with Jesse's band, but, when Jesse was billed to play a gig in February of 1970 with the Band, Jesse felt his group would provide a better contrast to the Band's full sound if he played with just himself and a bass player. So Ken was temporarily out of a job. It was just at this time that Janis was looking to form a new backup group.

Although Janis said that one of the reasons she left the second group was that she was always fighting the volume of the horns, she misses the punch that horns give her. "They gave me that umph when I needed it." But it's unlikely that her audience will miss them. John Till's lead guitar and Ken Pearson's organ filled in beautifully where the horn lines were, and they are a better harmonic match for her voice.

When Janis left Big Brother, it was like a marriage that had broken up, and ever since that time she had been looking for a partner that had the virtues of spontaneity and freshness without being amateurish. Her new group came as close to that as time allowed. If they were not quite what Big Brother was to Janis, it was perhaps because they were not part of the original Panhandle Park mythology. But as musicians they are more together than Big Brother. Also, Janis related to them: "These guys are on the same wavelength as me," Janis says "It's more of a family thing again."

John Till (lead) and Brad Campbell (bass) are the only two members Janis took with her from the last band. Brad had been with the second band since the beginning, but John joined Janis toward the end, playing rhythm guitar. He is a subtle and fast blues guitarist who started with Ronnie Hawkins' band three years ago when he got out of high school.

"Ronnie likes to get you real young and brainwash you. He'll make you think you couldn't play with anyone else even if you wanted to, and then he puts you in a black suit and a store-bought haircut, and you just stay there until you've got the guts to pull out." Brad, who played bass in the last group came from the now defunct Paupers (also managed by Albert Grossman) where he replaced Denny Gerard, and his bass is a solid match for Clark Pierson's drumming.

Richard Bell (piano) also came from Ronnie Hawkins' band, and both he and John Till backed the legendary Canadian harp player and singer King Biscuit Boy, otherwise known as Richard Newall. Bell's piano is both honky-tonky and jazzy and is a light improvisational element in a group that is heavily rhythmic. Richard was in college when Hawkins offered him "$50 a week and his laundry" and gave him 30 seconds to make up his mind. He took it. For all the weird stories attached to his name, Ronnie Hawkins, like a Canadian John Mayall, seems to have attracted and developed an incredible number of really talented musicians.

All the members of Full Tilt are Canadians, except for Clark Pierson, who played drums with Linn County. Janis had discovered Clark playing in the house band of the Galaxy, a San Francisco topless club. His drumming has a funky, heavy bump and grind beat, a perfect match for Janis' raunchy voice. "You know, I've had drummers that used to go a-one, a-two, a-three . . ." says Janis. "Clark just slams right into it."

"They just weren't happening for me," Janis said about the second band. "They just didn't get me off. You know, I have to have the umph, I've got to *feel* it, because if it's not getting through to me, the audience sure as hell aren't going to feel it either. This band is solid, their sound is so heavy you could lean on it, and that means I can go further out, and extend myself. It's together, man, that's what it is!"

—David Dalton, "Janis Joplin's Full Tilt Boogie Ride," *Rolling Stone*, August 6, 1970

Thy Alabaster Cities Gleam, Undimmed by Human Tears

AIRPORTS ALWAYS look desolate in spite of the crowds, which, I suppose, contributes to the profoundly dislocating sensation involved in traveling by air across America. I should say, the *illusion* of traveling, because essentially everywhere is the same for this superficial passenger. His adventures are hardly likely to be revealing. This disagreeable disenchantment comes from the horrible realization that you are tunneling from one vacuum to another. On the surface every city seems to be a replica, as if some city-hungry mantis had been there just before you and left behind him only a repellant, ambivalent husk.

Arriving in Kansas City or Memphis, you wonder where are the great mythic America cities, the bawdy frontier towns and slinky riverboat ports. You listen pointlessly for their breath, and, a little remorsefully, realize that these historical behemoths who once roamed our continent, massive as bison, have been reduced to dull, sluggish sows with regular habits by Circe's technocratic wand.

The airport is unmoved even by our bizarre band passing now through its intestines. It greets us, as it does every new arrival, with the mindless cheerfulness of a freshly scrubbed corpse. Everything here is a mischievous illusion, a Mission Impossible hoax in the synthetic colon of the universe. And yet the terrible irony that all of this has been constructed very deliberately remains. In its own way it is a miracle of American ingenuity. It must be reassuring to someone. But to whom?

The Avis girl smiles at us predictably as John Cooke gets the transportation together. The rest of us moon about like zombies in the white, blank waiting areas, sliding about the finely polished funerary floors.

Only Janis knows what to do with the time, plunks herself down, uncorks a bottle and sucks away blatantly on it to the amazed glares of the surrounding businessmen and several pathetic straggling family groups. Their potential hostility is generated by its absurdity alone.

In this context, Janis suddenly seems gargantuan, profoundly real. She looms among the shifting shades with a majestic density of being, as if she were descended from an almost extinct race of giants. She had this quality of making people disappear by comparison with her, a quality that, while necessary to her own psychic equilibrium, could be crushing to outsiders. Her ballsiness, of course, and tough, butch, gin-mama contortions did well

to sheathe the soft, brittle zone of her vulnerable core.

These collisions with the natives were almost theatrical, often with an element of farce, because Janis made everywhere she was her own stage, and if you stepped onto the boards you were obliged to perform. Sometimes they were a little less funny. The greatest possible insult, after all, is to question someone else's reality—something Janis did instinctively under hostile conditions. Her presence seemed to corrode everything other people took for granted, and for this reason most of the ridiculing, pointing, giggling impromptu audience held their distance. For them, exposure to Janis had the disturbing effect of seeing an anti-matter particle of themselves oscillating wildly in a dangerous proximity. To approach too closely meant the possibility of some kind of personal detonation.

She represented everything they hated and weren't allowed to be, curled into a saucy, flaunting ball of insolence. She scooped up all the hidden, grubby trash that had accumulated in their airless domes and shoved it at them like a huge smell. She created such catastrophic interferences and voids that they were bound to seek revenge with all their spiteful bourgeois talents. The crowning outrage was that she was not only fucking them, she was doing it in broad daylight, and the indiscretion seemed all the more flagrant in these immacultate, sterile spaces.

Janis was, for the most part, oblivious to their rays, because she carried around her own space with her into which she could retire. . . . Amid all the indigestible flux of these places she would sing little snatches of old songs to herself, like personal incantations against contamination with the environment. Usually they were not the kind of things she'd sing on stage—Merle Haggard, old Bessie Smith Numbers, and her favorite, a crazy formless little ditty called "It's

Life," which didn't have the slightest connection with Sinatra's glib rubric.

"What's life?"
"It's only a magazine."
"How much does it cost?"
"It only costs a quarter."
"Twenty-five cents? I've only got a nickel."
"That's life. . . ."

She was a bedbug in this synthetic universe, Mother Courage barreling through hell with her wagonload of goodies, her sons tagging along behind. "If only we could find some peace and quiet where there's no shooting going on, me and my kids, what's left of 'em—we could rest up for a while."

You couldn't help wondering if all this grandiose asceticism in which Janis plumped herself down, as ripe as a pear in August, was not at its root a form of anti-magic, a bane against accumulated apprehensions that made up a monstrous, self-inflicted lemure which flapped vindictively over a thousand years. Janis dangled her sweaty feet insolently in these antiseptic wards.

In the airport bar, decked out like the Garden of Allah, a gray executive from the local Coke convention with his identicard label pinned on the lapel, lunges at Janis like a dog appraising a building: "Hey, baby, you turned into a turtle yet?"

Janis looks defiantly into his cold blue Donald Duck eyes: "When I want you in my pond, you asshole, I'll let you know," she says slamming him with her Kozmic left hook, and he reels away into a pile of stale wisecracks.

Later, I naïvely asked Janis if he'd been talking about "Turtle Blues." "No, man," she said. "He was just being jive. He was just trying to be a smart ass. A lot of people do that. They'll challenge you once to see if you've got the balls to look like that. And you know, if you go 'Oooh, I'm sorry . . . uh, weel . . . egad . . .'—you know you're shot down already."

I'm Just Like a Turtle That's Hiding Underneath His Horny Shell

It is perfectly true, as the philosophers say, that life must be understood backwards. But they forget the other proposition, that it must be lived forwards. And if one thinks over that proposition it becomes more and more evident that life can never be understood in time simply because at no particular moment can one find the necessary resting place from which to understand it—backwards.
—Kierkegaard, *Journals,* 1843

IN THE LONG HOURS that precede the show few things relieve the monotony. We are in a drab high-ceilinged dressing room with one bare light bulb. Janis is making faces at herself in the mirror. Time is spent mainly stringing her beads. Great Mother Weaver of the World at her endless task. Oddly shaped pieces of glass and stone, slipping knots, tying off loose ends. Each strand represents hours and days of boredom, waiting . . . waiting, passing of time. Each stone marks an hour, each knot a minute eaten up. The beads have their own syntax, totally unconscious, the language of detached fingers, emptied of thoughts, automatic, repetitious. Perhaps if we could read them like a rosary they'd tell a lot. Interior verbs and nouns of glass and string speaking of opaque body rhythms.

Then comes the ritual of the bracelets, its incredible formality. The procedure is almost Tunisian in its intensity. Their elaborate shining rings glint in the harsh light of the tiny cubicle like the host of white birds that flew up after the birth of Cuchulain, each with a silver yoke between them. The weight of all that ripe amber and silver metal! It must feel like carrying a spare arm around. Silver tinkling circles overlapping, crowding, burying each other. It's hard to believe they don't serve some religious function. Janis slips on each one deliberately like feathery thin armor. Perhaps they do protect her in some way as she steps nightly into her own arena. It's not that the audience are cannibals, though in a sense they are that too, because the battle is really for them, with them against all the dull, wrongheaded specters that have cropped up during the day in fat wartlike growths.

And after the rapturous delusive trance that she will perform for them, freeing all the spirits of play and generation, breathing a wild heady air secreted like a magic chemical, the hard, callous folds of mental skin will inevitably grow back again. The performance is illusory, and the relief she will give them, like the yearly flight of the queen bee, is only a momentary ecstasy. But this frenzied meeting and hum of weightlessness is something that Janis needs too; the conspiracy is mutual, otherwise the repetitions would be murderous. Every night the same pretense at paradise, the same whirring ascension, the intoxication lingering a little while before its predictable sinking back into grim little banalities. The conditions of this act fall on both sides; Janis, too, must return to earth and often go home alone to a vacant motel room.

During these endless hours Janis occasionally reminisces. But somehow the histories reveal only one thing: the itinerary of her myth. She does not consciously hide the secret, wounded places, but a habit protects her. We will never know her true interior journey. The lapses into its painful stations are only revealing on a certain level. The deeper its story seems to penetrate her past, the more static the images it dredges up.

Its traces are engraved. You have the feeling that her childhood is hidden even from herself. Trunks of memories and clues of which the keys have been melted down years ago. We are only permitted to see her life as a geologic fault. From the other side, from her parents, a certain kind of truth emerges, more static, more hoped for and projected than perceived, and from here, from this side we see only what has *become* of a source, the monument stained by events, but in one sense it is more real, more focused than any life could actually be. The evolution of a star, her own program. It is a matter of indifference what the components of this myth are. As time passes we will leave its soft amorphous details further and further behind. This is as Janis would have wished it.

The truth is that the *facts* of a life that we pursue with missionary zeal are only signals from the great wastes. Our responses can only echo hollowly through these diffused experiences. Eventually we are forced to see the point. Janis is not dealing in signals. A signal, a fact, a scratch on the field of time is a reduction, a mere resonance of the monotonous physical universe. If anything, Janis wanted her life to be read in meanings, as a world of symbols in opposition to a world of noise.

The historical reality is totally unimportant. In fact Janis's whole life was spent erasing herself on this level and replacing it with myth. The actual memories of the events call across this giant fissure of time and space like the voices calling to each other across the river at the end of *La Dolce Vita*.

Can we talk about the past, Janis?

Past, yes, past.

How did Chet Helms find you?

I was in a hillbilly band, mostly hanging out —I was supposed to be going to college, but I just went up there so I could get it on. I was singing in this hillbilly group called the Waller Creek Boys—Waller Creek runs right through Austin—Pal St. John was in the group and a young guy called Lanny Williams who got married and had babies. We used to sing at this place called the Ghetto and just hang out and get drunk a lot, get in big fights, roll in the mud, drink beer and sing, pick and sing, pick and sing. Walked around carrying my autoharp. Never went anywhere without my autoharp. We were singing at this bar called Threadgills on the outskirts of town. It was a reconverted gas station, it still had that awning and everything, you'd pull the car in and go in and have a beer, and Mr. Threadgill was a hillbilly singer. Every Saturday night everybody would go there. It

was a very strange amalgam of people. There were all these old Okies, all the kids, little grand kids. Then there were a bunch of college professors—older cats that were into country music intellectually—the first of the folk trend, and then there were the young upstarts that were into it too, and that was us. And there was Mr. Threadgill—he surpassed them all. He was old, a great big man with a big belly and white hair combed back on the top of his head. And he was back there dishing out Polish sausages and hard-boiled eggs and Grand Prizes and Lone Star, "another 18 Lone Star" dishin out the Lone Star. And someone would say, "Mr. Threadgill, Mr. Threadgill, come out and do us a tune," and he'd say, "No, I don't think so," and they'd say, "Come on, come on," and he'd say, "All right." He'd close the bar down, and then he'd walk out front, and he'd lay his hands across his big fat belly, which was covered with a bar apron, just like in Duffy's Tavern. He'd come out like that and lean his head back and sing, just like a bird, Jimmie Rodgers songs, and he could yodel—God, he was fantastic. We used to go there and sing every Saturday, and I was the young upstart loudmouthed chick—"That girl sounds a lot like Rosie Maddox, don't she?" And I'd sing Rosie Maddox songs, and I'd sing Woody Guthrie songs, but one time an evening I'd say, "Can I do one now? Can I do one now?" and they'd say, "Okay, let that lady have a tune," and I'd say, "Give me a 12 bar in E." I sang blues, I could only sing one a night, I made it there every night. Chet heard me one weekend up there. He was famous, he was one of the crazies that made it away from Texas at a very early age, he had split at 18. He was back in town on the way to the West Coast from the East Coast—all Texans come back to Austin—and he heard me singing and he said, "That girl's good, that girl's good." I was wanting to leave, I was wanting to get the fuck out of here, but I didn't have quite enough nerve to leave by myself. Chet was leaving, and he said he wanted me to come with him and help him get rides. We hitchhiked to San Francisco, and we slept on a bunch of people's floors, and I sang a couple of times. I wasn't really that interested in singing, to tell you the truth, I had a couple of opportunities, I just wasn't that serious about anything, I was just a young chick, I just wanted to get it on. I wanted to smoke dope, take dope, lick dope, suck dope, fuck dope, anything I could lay my hands on I wanted to do it, man. Singing, singing just sort of faded out of my life, and I went through a number of personal changes—drug problems, heavy drug problems—and ended up back in Texas trying to get myself together, and I couldn't stand it down there. But I was afraid if I came back here I'd get fucked up again. I had been down here about

a year, which was just enough time for me to get really sick of it. How I really got in the band, it was really funny, it was perfectly apropos, because I hadn't been laid in a year, man, because who are you going to fuck in Port Arthur? I was down there trying to kick, not getting fucked, trying to get through college, because my mother wanted me to, and I was in Austin doing a little folk-music gig, playing the guitar, and this old boyfriend of mine came—this cat I used to make it with—this was years after I left Austin, it was '65, and I left in '61. I had gone to the big city and got good and evil and came back home, with a little R 'n' R, right? This cat came down, and I was playing a gig, and after the gig I was over at some people's house, and I was sitting there, and this cat came in and *scooped* me right up, man, it was Travis. Travis just came and *scooped* me up, threw me onto the bed, whoo, baby! He just fucked the livin shit out of me all night long! Fucked me all night long!, fucked me all morning. I was feeling so good—you know how chicks are in the morning—a cop-out. (*A high chick's voice*) "Well, hi!" (*Low man's voice*) "What is it?" He said, "Go get your clothes, I think we're going to California." I said, "Okay." Halfway through New Mexico I realized I'd been conned into being in the rock business by this guy that was such a good ball. I said, "Well it's bound to be, man." I was fucked into being in Big Brother. But after I got here and started singing I really loved it. So I got to San Francisco and met all these strange guys. Chet knew me, and Chet was managing Big Brother. Chet had sent Travis down to try and talk me into being the center of his group, because he thought I was a good singer and would make it, but I had never got it together. He happened to hit me at the right time, and I came out to be in a group, but I didn't know it. While I was gone, and I'd been in Texas for a long time, but when I was leaving George Hunter was putting a show together. There was no rock and roll in those days—it was '64 when I left—George was talking about putting me in a rock and roll band, and he had this poster, the first rock and roll poster. George Hunter drew it, it said, "The Amazing Charlatans." I used to have it on my wall and go, "Far out, what have these crazy boys done now?" I came back to San Francisco, and rock and roll had happened. Well, I'd never sung rock and roll, I sang blues—Bessie Smith kind of blues. They said, "Janis, we want you to sing with these boys," and I met them all, and you know how it is when you meet someone, you don't even remember what they look like you're so spaced by what's happening, I was in space city, man. I was scared to death. I didn't know how to sing the stuff, I'd never sung with electric music, I'd never sung with drums, I only sang with one guitar. We finally did the song "Down On Me." I learned "Down On Me." It's a gospel song, and I'd heard it before and thought I could sing it, and they did the chords. So we practiced it all week, and they were working at the Avalon that weekend. They played a few numbers, and then they said, "Now we'd like to introduce . . ." and nobody had ever heard of fuckin me, I was just some chick, didn't have any hip clothes or nothing like that, I had on what I was wearing to college. I got on stage, and I started singing, whew! what a rush, man! A real live drug rush. I don't remember it at all, all I remember is the sensation—what a fuckin gas, man. The music was boom, boom, boom! and the people were all dancing, and the lights, and I was standing up there singing into this microphone and getting it on, and whew! I dug it. So I said, "I think I'll stay, boys." Far out, isn't it? It sure did take *me* by surprise, I'll tell you. I wasn't planning any of this, I wasn't planning on sitting in cold dressing rooms all my life, I didn't even know it ex-

isted. Even when I was a singer I never wanted to be a star. I just liked to sing because it was fun, just like people like to play tennis, it makes your body feel good. Everybody gave you free beer. I don't remember much of the early period, we just worked around, all of us starving, I got some money from my parents. . . .

I could have met Otis Redding twenty times and married him, but once I saw him on stage, he's a star, man. I've never been that close to a star.

You're a star, Janis.

That's different . . . and besides, I haven't accepted that kind of thing yet. You can't say you are a star. I know me, I've been around a long time, I've been this chick for twelve, thirteen years now. I was younger then, more inexperienced, but I was the same person with the same drives and the same balls and the same style. I was the same chick, because I've been her forever, and I know her, she ain't no star—she's lonely, or she's good at something. I have to get undressed after the show, my clothes are ruined, my heels are run through, my underwear is ripped, my body's stained from my clothes, my hair's stringy, I got a headache and I got to go home and I'm lonely, and my clothes are all fucked up, my shoes have come apart, and I'm pleading with my road manager to please give me a ride home, please, please, just so I can take these fuckin clothes off, and that ain't no star, man, that's just a person. I have one thing I can do, and I'm getting better at it, too, which makes me proud. It makes you feel like an artist rather than a fluke, man, which I think I was. I just happened to have the right combination at the right time. But now I am learning how and that's my job to improve, and I am, and that makes me feel good. Everybody can do something at some time, but people aren't interested in what one person can do, and pass by and always be a loser, but in another place and time they just may come to you, and that doesn't mean you're any better than anybody else. So many people don't try, I mean people who really fuckin try to be fair and to be good at what they do, they really fuckin work, they're artists, in artistic bands, they really try. But I was just lucky, and I know how lucky I am, because I've been down, and I had the same beads on and the same "hi ya boys" style so that I can get laid. Don't tell me I'm a star, man.

"You Left Me Here to Face It All Alone"

MORNINGS WERE always the worst for Janis, tired and sodden, gluing herself together on the spur of the moment for the trip to the airport. Some mornings she looked as if she'd been run over in her sleep. Like a moth brutally caught in a blinding light, she staggered out of her motel room into the cruel glare of the early afternoon.

Pain seeped into her by day and evaporated at night. First thing in the morning, even the Southern Comfort tastes bitter. It was close to a chemical infection. All this bred a low-grade despair in her that fell into her head like water tapping at the bottom of a deep well in which she could see herself as clearly as the grotesque reflections that suddenly appear at the bottom of a glass.

Even her fatalism, ultimately relaxing, and her personal store of wisdom could not brace her against the blows when they came. Comfort is made of compromises, and Janis would have no part of its nasty cycle. The paralysis of Kozmical despair seemed to be at the very center of her everyday life. Like a virus that has penetrated too deeply, she carried around with her the weight of this reali-

zation that finally crushed her with all the mysterious forms that despair gives rise to. She carried the Troubled Truth about like the goat carrying the mountain in a wry Sufi fable.

It is called the Troubled Truth for good reason, for while it is certain of being the truth, it is troubled as to what to do with it, out of a concern that others might not accept it. Would Poco, for instance, who were traveling on the tour, with their fresh, wide-eyed, psychedelic innocence, accept this knowledge of the real pain of the world that had been served up to Janis in microcosm?

At bottom it had something to do with entropy's terrible whine, and therefore, by inference the Kozmic Blues, but Janis came to know that as long as she stared at her plate she could not solve it, nor would it go away. Again, what to do with it? Even the more sensitive members of Full Tilt would probably not understand it, and it was hardly an appetizing gift, this bundle of wounded intentions wrapped up like a dead thing.

Alcohol and drugs became the obvious conspirators in the *causa sui* project, magical partners hired only for a time and at collosal expense to put to sleep the overwhelming odds.

Her personal pain sat squatly on her life; its purposiveness did not seem to be diminished by time. It wasn't that others couldn't see it at all, although the more subtle truths about Janis could only be grasped by those with the power to identify with it. Most people who did glimpse it thought it was a better idea to ignore it. But it was there just the same, a lump of pain, like a black mucus, glued onto her since childhood. All efforts to remove it, transplant it, or exorcise it proved futile. It could only be temporarily shifted. In the midst of the most raucous occasions it would pop up insolently to mock any attempt to still it.

Janis could see quite clearly into her own

murky depths with chilling perception; in fact, her perception of it only compounded the pain. In spite of this, she was always puzzled by her inability to solve her own riddle.

If Janis saw that her personal happiness was illusory, it was not because she had not thought about it and worked it out as best anyone could from both ends (mind and body), but it still hadn't helped. The worst of it was in the fact that it *wasn't* a personal problem at all; it was just that in her secret way she took the responsibility for it. The Great Saturday Night Swindle was simply a condition of the world, *that* was what was so depressing about it. When you *know,* the pain becomes intolerable. As Lennon said: "If you don't *know,* man, then there's no pain." A kind of incipient fatalism took hold in Janis, not exactly a cynical philosophy, just an inverted blessing to hold back the flood. It wasn't that Janis wouldn't have given a lot to be just a *little bit* cynical, to cut away just some of the weight, to turn a bit of it loose: "Untie me, god of knots!"

The idea of analysis did not, however, appeal to her either. In quaint Southern camp she referred to analysts as "special doctors." The previous winter in L.A., Arthur Janov handed me a copy of *The Primal Scream* to give to Janis. He seemed genuinely concerned about her. He had been alerted to the fact, he said, that everything might not be right with her from the bloodcurdling screams she let out on her records and in her performances. To him they seemed like unmistakable, hard, crystalline nuggets of Pain. "She is so close to having a Primal," he said, "it's almost as if she were about to trigger it off in herself, but of course, she never will. I'd like to take her the whole way there." He had also heard through sources of his own (he was treating a considerable number of junkies at the time) that Janis was on smack, and therefore he was doubly anxious to help.

When I showed the book to Janis, later that year, she thumbed through it distractedly, said she'd check it out maybe when she got back to Larkspur "It's a *heavy* book, man," and besides, could *Zelda* live with it?

Janis's unhappy childhood, her limitless sadness, only precipitated these ideas into a hidden inwardness. Even her formidable myth, constructed like some opulent dream, could not quiet the gnawing evidence. After a certain point there was no going back, and at the worst of times these constructions and facades only helped to make things seem more hopeless than they actually were, as if personal storms had torn holes in all her grandiose sets leaving the punctured scrims to flap at her head mockingly while painful internal gusts ripped through her.

"Why Should I Be Afraid Since There Is Nothing Here But Me?"

Just say she was someone
So far from home
Whose life was so lonesome
She died all alone
Who dreamed pretty dreams
That never came true
Lord, why was she born
So black and blue
—Kris Kristofferson, "Epitaph (Black and Blue)"

FEW PEOPLE were closer to Janis than John Cooke. In answer to the somewhat heartless and melodramatic way her death was treated in *Rolling Stone,* he wrote: "There is not the slightest suspicion in my mind that her death might have been intentional. She didn't believe in cutting short a rocking good time, and that was what she was having."

Of course it *wasn't* suicide, but what was it? And does it matter anyway, now that

Janis is no bigger than the spot of blood that day on her new silk pants that Richard showed me in the photograph he'd taken of her in front of one of her twelve-foot posters outside the Albert Hall? I remember at the time that little decimal point stopped my circulation for a few congealed moments as I wondered about the body that didn't live quietly, just as it stopped again about a year later when I heard that that little dot had stung her for the last time.

"Who asked you to work your life away just trying to entertain us?" a chick from Boston wrote in one of the many angry, rhetorical letters addressed to Janis after her death. Its sincerity makes me wonder. Are they reading in heaven tonight?

A lot of people found it difficult to believe that if Janis's death wasn't suicide of the head, that maybe it was some other form of suicide. She saw it coming. The disappointment you could see in Janis's eyes sometimes could make you cry. Not when she was whining or bitching in her plaintive croaky voice, but sometimes when everything just seemed to overwhelm her and she just slumped in a pathetic heap on a beat-up sofa.

Was it just a form of romantic self-pity that made Janis, after Jimi had died, tell friends, among them her polar twin, Little Richard, "Goddammit, he beat me to it"?

The first time I heard anyone talk about the possibility of Janis's death was on the train trip across Canada. I was talking to someone in Delaney and Bonnie's band about following Janis around for a while and writing a book about it. "You'd better hurry up," he said. "She's not going to be around much longer." I was a little stunned, but I put it down to the kind of hip bravado that people put out as insight.

Anyway it seemed a very unlikely possibility. What could possibly do Janis in? She seemed as solidly situated on this earth as Mount Rushmore. I could even imagine her as an old lady, although I did not exactly see her as Lillian Roxon did in tweeds with a couple of strands of pearls—but I *could* see her clearly as a grandmother rocking on a porch somewhere.

It never occurred to me that it might be Janis herself who would do herself in. Of course, the equation was perfectly lethal. It only confirmed the fact that there'd been this incredibly vicious internal struggle going on all along.

Although it seems pitiless to say it, if she had not died this year or next, or in the next decade, and if she had not stopped drinking and doping and generally bribing the Hippocampal Gate with heavy doses of self-annihilation, Janis would probably have had to look forward to many grim years in hospitals and rest homes patching up her body as it gradually wore down under the strain.

The Grateful Dead grew up with Janis on the streets of Haight-Ashbury, played, and got stoned with her, and (a privilege granted to few others) let her get them drunk. Janis died during "Cold Rain and Snow" in the Dead's set at Winterland. Jerry Garcia, with the affection of an old friend, looked her death in the face stoically:

"Like everybody does it, the way they do it. Death only matters to the person that's dying. The rest of us are going to live without that voice. For those of us for whom she was a person, we'll have to do without the person.

"Janis was like a *real person,* man. She went through all the changes we did. She went on all the same trips. She was just like the rest of us—fucked up, strung out, in weird places. Back in the old days, the presuccess days, she was using all kinds of things, just like anybody, man.

"When she went out after something, she went out after it really hard, harder than most people ever think to do, ever conceive of doing.

"She was on a real hard path. She picked it, she chose it, it's OK. She was doing what she was doing as hard as she could, which is as much as any of us can do. She did what she had to do and closed her books. I don't know whether it's *the* thing to do, but it's what she had to do.

"It was the best possible time for her death. If you know any people who passed that point into decline, you know, really getting messed up, old, senile, done in. But going up, it's like a skyrocket, and Janis was a skyrocket chick.

"She had a sense of all that, including the sense that if somebody was making a movie of it, it'd make a great movie. If you had a chance to write your life . . . I would describe that as a good score in life writing, with an appropriate ending."

God it gets so lonely
when the fire is in your veins
when all ya' got is one
last shot
to get it right again

From "Sheila" by Eric Anderson

PART TWO

The Mechanics of Ecstasy

Upon the planes of ritual, ecstasy and meta-physics, ascension is capable, among other things, of abolishing Time and Space and of ''projecting'' man into the mythical instant of the Creation of the World, whereby he is in some sense ''born again,'' being rendered con-temporary with the birth of the World . . . when existence and Time first became mani-fest. . . . The radical ''cure'' of the suffering of existence is attained by retracing one's foot-steps in the sand of memory.

—Mircea Eliade, *Myths, Dreams and Mysteries*

THE MECHANICS OF ECSTASY

Backstage Louisville

LADY REPORTER: Do you drink before going on stage?

JANIS: I never drink until right before I go on. If I drink three or four hours before I go on, an hour before I go on, plus while I'm on I'm not gonna enjoy the show because I'm not gonna remember it, and I decided a couple of weeks ago that the music sounded so good that I wanted to be there, man. People used to tell me, "Wow, you did this and that," and I'd say, "Wow, it sounds great, I wish I'd been there."

DAVID: The band sounds great, really right there.

JANIS: Honey, honey, I'm telling you, they're great, man, I'm so fuckin proud of them, I'm just so jacked to work with them, every day I just kiss 'em and tell 'em I love 'em, man. It's better than it's ever been for me. They're right behind me, they *follow* me, do you notice? when I go down they go "bop," when I go up they go "bop, bop, bop," they're so great. Really big talent.

LADY REPORTER: How did you find them?

JANIS: Oh, here and there. Albert found some of them for me, some of them met somebody else.

DAVID: How come you changed from horns?

JANIS: Volume. Too many people complained there was too much noise. I like having horns, man, I like having the punch that horns give you, but they're too much trouble on the road, too much noise, too much crowding on stage, it just didn't work out. I like working with horns because it really gives you that "pow!" I really need it, man, but there's all those Tuesday mornings in the hotel, people not showing up when they're supposed to.

LADY REPORTER: What do people say when you wear those clothes in hotels and restaurants?

JANIS: Yeah, they're real rude to me, they treat me like someone they don't want in there, and they don't want me in there. But it depends on how hard they are. You can leave and say "Fuck them, I don't have to take this," or you show them your money, and they allow you to stay. Everybody who looks weird gets fucked over. I look pretty weird, but I do the best I can.

DAVID: Why do people want to fight with people who look weird?

JANIS: I guess it's that whole thing you hear about, because they're scared, that's what they're trying to say is because they don't like you is why, but why they don't like you I don't know. Whether it's a reasonable reason or whether it's hung-up prejudice reason, maybe their son is dropping acid, or maybe they think you're trying to hold up the banks. Basically, it's because you're on a different trip from them.

DAVID: I think they say, "I'm not allowed to look like that, how come they can get away with it?" Don't you think?

JANIS: Maybe so. Maybe they just don't like your fuckin ass.

LADY REPORTER: Are you a pessimistic person?

JANIS: Aaaaahhh, I used to think so. I was a real pessimist, a real cynical bitch. Then I read somewhere this definition that said "A pessimist is never disappointed, and an optimist is constantly let down." So by that definition I'd be an optimist. But I consider myself rather cynical. . . . They called me a fine feathered bird last week, "Here comes the fine feathered bird."

LADY REPORTER: Who said that?

JANIS: Oh, .a friend of mine, one of my crazy friends.

She leaves. Janis asks me what do I think she'll write.

That chick? I know she's gonna write a good thing.

"You never can tell," Janis says cynically. "Sometimes they think they're gonna like you and then you get out there and you really damage and offend their femininity. You know, "No chick is supposed to stand like *that.*" You know, your tits shakin around, and your hair's stringy, and you have no makeup on, and sweat running down your face, and you're coming up to the fuckin microphone, man, and at one point their heads just go click, and they go "Oooh, no." You get that a lot, it's really far out, when you're standing on stage you can't see the whole crowd. The trouble is the groovy crowd is usually in the back, because they can't afford the seats down front—the seats down front are the local rich people—and they're the ones that are just sitting there, man, with their knees just so . . . and you know, you only cross at your ankles, keep your panty girdle tight together, and you sit with your hands in your lap, and I'm up there singing, I'm going "Cha-cha-boom-quack-quack,"

and I look out at the crowd, and these girls have these little pinched smiles on their faces, and I must be an absolute *horror,* man, they've never seen anything like it, and they don't want to again, man. The chick's up there, shakin it all, "How do you like that, boys," and the boys all go "Aaaaaaghhh!" [*verbal equivalent of an R. Crumb drool*] and the girls are going "Oh, my God, she may be able to sing, but she doesn't have to act like that." That's the way I was raised, man, I know exactly what's on those bitches' minds, they don't like me, man. But that's not most of them, I figure most of them who go to the trouble to buy a ticket to come to my shows are ready to rock.

A lot of chicks in the audience are really behind you.

Yeah, but that's the trouble, the lights, you can't see them.

A lot of chicks really identify with you.

At my concerts most of the chicks are looking for liberation, they think I'm gonna show 'em how to do it. But the ones right in the front are always the country club bitches, they always are. It's so *weird* playing to 14 panty girdles. I used to get really uptight when they turned on the house lights because I thought it would cool the show, but I noticed in the past year it doesn't. You turn on the house lights, and if you've got an audience that's a little timid the minute they see everybody else standing up and getting goony, they say, what the fuck, and everybody just stands up and starts getting sweaty. I used to think if they couldn't see me singularly and watch me turn them on, they wouldn't get turned on, but now I know if they can see each other get turned on, they're gonna get turned on even more. The fact that I look small and human like I do when the lights are on don't matter one fuckin bit.

I'm a strong believer in magic. I'd fly across the country to see Otis for ten minutes. I'd go see Little Richard anywhere, I'd go see Tina anywhere, because they *work,* they *happen,* they're *electric,* they're *exciting,* they sweat for you. Fuck, they're so great, man, I just love 'em.

DAVID: Otis was great, when he came on stage he was like a flash of lightning.

JANIS: It's what I tell the boys, it's what Sly's band is good at—what you're seeing up there is rhythm, you're going "Chug-a-chug-a-chug-a-chug." Well, with those good groups you not only feel that rhythm, you not only hear it, but you see it. Like Otis, whenever he walked, he walked in time—"Got-to-get-my-got-to-get-chug-a-chug." Sly does it, too—"Higher, higher." They *move,* they make the song visible, you feel like your whole brain is just one 1–2–3–4 rhythm.

JOHN COOKE [*in a nasal delivery-boy tone*]: Western Union, ma'am. They're just starting an underground press in this town, and there's a young man here with long hair from the underground press who wants to talk to you.

JANIS: Is he sexy?

JOHN: Well, I don't know, I'm not a connoisseur of young men. There's some nice-looking little girls out there, but they're all jailbait. So what do I tell this guy? Tell him you don't ever want to see him?

JANIS: Tell him I'll answer a few questions, I don't want to do an interview.

HIPPIE REPORTER: What do you expect the concert to come off like tonight?

JANIS: I think it's gonna be double dynamite, man. I'm planning on having a good time.

HIPPIE: There's a Southern Comfort and Ripple party tonight in your honor.

JANIS: *Whooooo!*

HIPPIE: What do you think of Louisville now that you've seen it?

JANIS: I haven't seen it. I've been from the airport to the hotel, and the hotel to the bar, and the bar to the room and the room to here.

HIPPIE: How long have you been on the road now?

JANIS: This tour? Not long. I don't look so good, man. I look tired. I don't mind if I'm on stage. You know, it's funny, like most girls I'm always really self-conscious about do I look too fat, if my legs are short, if I'm weird shaped, but when I go on stage, man, it never even occurs to me. I think I look beautiful.

HIPPIE: Are you back with Big Brother?

JANIS: Oh, no!

[*The hippie reporter leaves a few minutes later.*]

DAVID: You've got to be kind to your own people, you know.

JANIS: I'm not being kind?

DAVID: Yeah, you are, you're cool.

JANIS: He was scared, I could have been nicer, I should have been nicer, right? What am I supposed to do?

DAVID: Everyone is nervous when they come to see you, because you're such a star.

JANIS: I can't relate to that, I can't relate to that. If they know anything about anything, they know I'm not a star. They know I'm a middle-aged chick with a drinking problem, man, and a loud voice, and other things, too, but, you know, fuck, there ain't nothing special about that.

DAVID: What you do on stage is a complete mystery. . . .

JANIS: I don't get it, and I don't believe it. I just can't get it conceptually.

DAVID: Even Mick doesn't get up on stage and get into the music like that. That's fantastic, you have to be right there to do that. He takes two or three numbers to warm up, the first time he's self-conscious and putting himself on, but when you do it, it's incredible.

JANIS: Well, I can't relate to that. False modesty, man.

DAVID: Well, let's put it down to that.

JANIS: Fuck you.

DAVID: Also, people are intimidated by you because you're such a large figure.

JANIS: I lost a lot of weight.

DAVID: I'm talking about symbolically.

JANIS: I'm just fucking with you, man.

DAVID: Did he leave his notes here? You see how nervous he was.

JANIS: I know he was nervous, but what am I supposed to do, turn around and say, "I'm a person"?

DAVID: It's hard, but anyway, he went away thinking how great you are, because that's what he came here thinking.

JANIS: Why do they come and see me? I don't know what they want to know.

DAVID: They just want to see you, you're such a star.

JANIS: Pshaw! No, I don't think I'm a star. I'll never be a star like Jimi Hendrix or Bob Dylan, I figured out why—cause I tell the truth. If they want to know who I am, they ask me and I'll tell them.

Unlike the blues singers whom Janis admired and emulated—Bessie Smith and Billie Holiday—Janis was not a classic blues singer. To some she took the blues farther than they had ever gone, and to others she contaminated a classic form with wretched excesses. But, her blues were of another order altogether, which precludes comparisons. This is perhaps why so much inarticulate (and articulate) fury was generated by these pointless comparisons.

Few of the numinous singers of the 60's had what would be called "good" voices. Vocal polishing is more an element of the 50's, and those groups who did achieve it—the Beach Boys, the Four Seasons, the Mamas and the Papas—do not fit in easily with the mainstream of 60's folk heroes from Dylan to the Stones. It's almost as if that articulation of harmony and manicured vocal inflection was too produced, its surface too smooth, with nothing to hook onto.

Heroes from the past were also elected with little regard to purity: Chuck Berry, Bo Diddley, Howlin' Wolf, and Little Richard. All dirty, "gutsy" singers.

You could almost say that this unconditioned, unpolished quality of rock is its most tangible feature. "My music is not a cerebral trip. It's nothing without guts. I don't worry about whether it's musical, but it did get off!" Janis said with subjective precision.

Reviewing "Pearl" in *Rolling Stone* Jack Shadoian wrote:

Her last album can't simply be an occasion for evaluation. The fact that there will be no more studio albums inevitably outweighs the issue of how good or how bad the record might be. Besides, Janis was a heavy, and had incredible presence whether at the top or bottom of her form. She was a remarkable, if erratic, singer, and she proved it, live and on record. Anyone who exhibits qualities of greatness earns certain privileges—not critical immunity so much as the right to be forever removed from inconsequentiality: all their work, flawed or not, is worth experiencing. Would you rather listen to bad Monk or good Ramsey Lewis? Or, if Monk could ever be called bad, could Lewis ever be called good? In certain instances, "good" and "bad" can be pretty useless terms. It's Janis, or it's Monk, and you listen, and you care, because you know that whatever is going down is genuine and may contain a revelation, and possibility that may be written off in the case of lesser artists.

On the Knees of the Heart

Natives widely believe that the essence of a person, song, object resides within, not on the surface, not in outward appearances. . . .

From this comes the belief that although the world consists of bodies, each contains within itself an essence, power, vital energy, which under certain conditions is given out, illuminating, changing whatever it touches. When such energy meets forces radiating from another

Telegram

western union

```
LD68 BG PDF   LOUISVILLE KY 702P JUN 12

JANICE JOPLIN DLY .75

   CARE BOX OFFICE STATE FAIR AND EXPOSITION CENTER
   FREEDOM HALL LVILLE

WELCOME WE INVITE YOU TO A SOUTHERN COMFORT AND RIPPLE

PARTY TONIGHT AFTER YOUR PERFORMANCE AT THE FREE PRESS

OFFICE LOVE.

      THE FREE PRESS STAFF 1438 SOUTH FIRST FREE UNION OF
      COLLECTIVE KARMA AND THE YIP YIP WATERMELON TRIBE
                              707P
```

WU 1201 (R 5-69)

being, something new may be created. Similarly, forces from other beings may penetrate one, enter one, change one. One may "drink in" another. Be possessed by another. Become *in*spired.
—Edmund Carpenter,
They Became What They Beheld

THE WORLD is so closed off, only a chink is left through which to see what could be. All the pores are closed down, shut out. The performance is the only thing left. Only in these nightly explosions does the living breath really return. Eerily, it is also Janis's childhood, precipitated. No matter how dissipated-looking Janis got, on stage she always looked like the unicellular child: reckless, extreme, indulgent, and radiant, remaking the world in an hour in a hopelessly doomed project, Janis stretched it out to its absolute limit.

In this projection there is an almost superhuman effort involved, because the audience will only believe the dream if they can be made to see it as a true dream, and thereby to liberate within themselves the magic freedom of dreams. They will only recognize it when it's thrust upon them violently.

Janis's talent for dealing in collective

identities made such rushes all the more plausible. *Okay, Kansas, you and I are going to come to grips,* or what she said to a country deejay who had just stolen a kiss, "Honey, you just took on Port Arthur!" or what Janis said to J. Marks: "I just made love to 25,000 people, and I'm going home alone." On stage this habit of sweeping all these individual specks of pulverized appearances into a Leviathan was more concrete. The program consisted of using her intensity to weld together all the threads, scales, and traces of our collective person, as if she were piecing Humpty Dumpty back together again.

Through music's power of anarchic disassociation she let us know that only all of us can see it. Too vast to guess by parts and too enclosed in *us* for us to see it at all.

"Back in Port Arthur, I'd heard some Leadbelly records, and, well, if the blues syndrome is true, I guess it's true about me. So I began listening to blues and folk music. I bought Bessie Smith records, and Odetta and Billie Holiday . . ." Janis says, visiting herself.

Janis was funky but closer in style to Bessie Smith than to raunchier blues singers like Ma Rainey, who gravitated towards rough jazz band or solo guitar accompanists like Tampa Red. Bessie Smith preferred to be backed by a professional orchestra like Fletcher Henderson's.

Bessie's bows and tassels are in sharp contrast to Ma's necklace of twenty-dollar gold pieces or her pearls slung around her neck like tiny hard sacks of flour. There was something wistful about Bessie, and that was also in Janis. Bessie, too, like Janis, was more theatrical than the earthy country blues singers they emulated. They both enjoyed the delicious artificiality of the theater, where stars arrive on stage from a different dimension—"the wings," as they say. "Per-

formers," said the thief, in *The Children of Paradise,* "aren't 'people,' they're everybody at the same time."

"I'm Gonna Use It Till the Day I Die"

"EVEN THE ARTICULATE or brutal sounds of the globe, must be all so many languages and ciphers that somewhere have their corresponding keys—have their own grammar and syntax; and thus the least things in the universe must be secret mirrors to the greatest," said De Quincey in his *Autobiography.*

Freedom Hall, where the concert took place, is a monster indoor stadium designed for wrestling matches and basketball games, the kind of place that looks empty even when it's full to capacity. With an audience of about 4,000, it looked pretty sad. To make matters worse, the crowd, mostly younger kids in neat hippy/mod threads, did not *look* like Janis' crowd.

Janis took a peek between the curtains before going on and realized it was not exactly Angels' Night at the Avalon Ballroom.

It took a while for the audience to get into it, but Janis was having *her* party, and she was just waiting for them to come over.

"Some dance hall you got here," Janis said hand-on-hip, Bette Davis style. "You know, sometimes we go into a place and take a quick look at the hall, a quick look at the dressing rooms, and a quick look at the audience, and we say, well, if we're going to have a party here, we're going to have to do it ourselves . . ."

"Try Just a Little Bit Harder," a girl shouted out as a request, and Janis yelled back, "I beg your pardon, I'm doing *my* part, honey."

If things started slowly, the concert ended in a near-riot, and the rent-a-cops in their Mountie hats, not sure whether they were at a concert or a demonstration, blew their cool and began driving back the kids rushing the stage with their clubs and flashlights. Meanwhile Janis was ecstatic.

"I permit them to dance," she yelled to a burly sergeant-at-arms, "in fact, I demand it!" And the rent-a-cop marched up and down scowling and fuming and shaking his fist at Janis in a gesture of revenge, and for a minute, it looked like one of those movies about small Southern towns where the good-hearted rainmaker gets run out of town on the next train. But, in fact, everybody had a good time except the rent-a-cops, who couldn't figure out what role to play and ended up overacting.

It all started when Janis began to get into "Try," with her jive about, "Honey, if you've had your eye on a piece of talent and that chick down the road has been getting all the action, then you know what you gotta do . . ." and *wham!* the drum kicks into the song, and Janis lays on her message: "Try a little bit harder."

As she got into it, she jumped off the stage, and a kid in the front row started shaking it down with her. That was all that was needed. Everybody got out, onto, and over their chairs and stayed dancing, shouting and clapping.

From there things just kept grinding on with "Summertime," "Kozmic Blues" and "Move Over." By the time she got into her last number, "Piece of My Heart," security had all the house lights turned on in the hope that it would cool everybody out, but it had just the opposite effect. The kids saw that *everybody* was standing, dancing up and down and screaming, and it just made them wilder and eventually the whole audience swarmed up to the stage like a hive of bees.

In this conservative Southern town, it was as if Janis had flashed a vision of the Garden of Eden at them. And they didn't want it to end.

They were grateful to Janis for taking them away from where they were and putting their heads somewhere else, and they showed it. Janis was exhausted but excited; the rain dance had worked. As Janis and the band left the stage in the eternal rock pantomine of unplugging guitars, the crowd howled for more.

—*Rolling Stone*, August 6, 1970

Janis took another sip of Southern Comfort and hit into the encore. The first doomy notes of "Ball and Chain" on the guitar always told of their end with the inevitability of a pendulum, and as Janis wails into the last impossible notes you realize that they are outside of musical terms.

Janis's voice spews out in trills and shrieks, cries and moans, everything that was unresolved in her life. Whirring horrors let fly from a deep pit and wards of sorrow all attended and nursed to their ecstatic moments by fierce, volatile "head notes" that rush from every corner of the universe with

the dizzying trajectory of elementary particles to gather up all the monstrous, painful and pathetic sounds, human and subhuman, known and imagined, that can bear witness to the bottomless sadness that inhabited her. Noises full of real terror, the whining of dogs, the croaking of drains, blind helpless screams, shrieks of scraping metal, pitiful and cruel, are all given Janis's body from moment to moment and they toss her mercilessly. We are *made* to hear the pain: two voices struggle for possession in a cracked harmony, while an army of "i"s stabs the air with piercing points, and words pile up in stuttering hoarse clumps of confusion.

> Aaah *want* someone to tell me,
> got to tell me—
> whyiiiiiiiiiiii!
> Just because I got to want your luuuuv . . .
> Honeh, jus because I need, need, need your love
> I said, honey, I don't understand.
> B-b-b-b-but, honeh, I wanna chance to trrry
> i-i-i-i-i-i-i-i-i-i-i-i-i-i-i-I-I-I-I!
> try, try, try, try, tri-i-i-i-i!-huh-huh-huh-huh-i-i!

Little Richard called "the voices" with which Janis sang "a sign of her possession of the Holy Spirit which she brought with her out of the South." Even if we do not use these terms to describe the inhuman moans and shrieks she squeezed out of her body with shuddering violence, we believe that their waywardness and compulsiveness came from violent forces and secret causes that forced her soul into its own shape, "as certain ethereal Chemicals operate on the Mass of neutral intellect."

As if awakened by her own voice in a dream, Janis comes out of her trance and walks into a rap which is incredibly moving because of the totality of its correspondence: "I don't understand, how come . . . you're *gone*, man . . . I don't understand why half the world is still cryin' . . . when the other half of the world is still cryin', too, man, I can't get it together . . . I mean, if you got a cat for one day, man . . . and say, maybe you want a cat for 365 days . . . you ain't got him for 365 days . . . you got him for one day . . . well, I tell you, that one day, man, had better be your life . . . because you can say, oh, man, you can cry about the other 364 . . . but you're gonna lose that one day, man, and that's all you got . . . you gotta call that love, man . . . that's what it is, man . . . if you got it today you don't want it tomorrow, man . . . cause you don't need it . . . cause, as a matter of fact, to-morrow never happens, man, it's all the same fuckin day. . . ."

The only reference point is Janis and then to us in the degree with which we participate. We are invited to follow their dizzying, pain-ful flight, or remain pinned to our fixed states, as the Big Open Notes take off on their journey through space, flying past at the speed of light. At first they are so con-cerned about their destination that they don't realize what they are traveling in. The capsule of sound is constantly shifting, its outline is as familiar to them as a Terra-plane, or an old Plymouth. "If you keep this up we're going to have an accident," says a sharp E chord from "After You've Gone." Suddenly they realize that it is none of these, it is more the *idea* of a car they are traveling in and all the notes jiggling, dancing and fly-ing around them with the indecisiveness of cartoons are just as much the *idea* of a high-way, and as they feel themselves, a little late, slamming on the brakes, they know they have crashed blissfully through the other side of Everything.

hah-hah-hah-hah-huhn-hhaaaahaaaahhhaaahaaaah
   hold on like it's the last moment of your life, because
     some day
a weight's gonna come on your shoulders babeh
and it's gonna feel just like a ball . . .
Anuhnananananuhn-hauhnhahahuhn-
   nananuhnananuhn-ni-i-i-i-i-uuuhn
chayayayayayayayayayayn!

Bar Talk

WHEN IT CAME to bars Janis was absolutely fearless—she would walk in anywhere. It was her way of touching ground; she'd plunk herself down at the bar, a heel hooked around the rail and elbow crooked in the padded ledge, as if to keep her from drifting away.

In spite of the alcoholic fraternity of such places, Janis was always alert, an acolyte in the service of Fields's devotional equation: "When you woo a wet goddess, there's no use falling at her feet." She would become repe-titious and ornery but rarely foggy or boring, and it was amazing, therefore, how often she tolerated the most incredibly maudlin, ob-noxious drinking partners.

I came down one morning to find Janis settled into the motel bar as if it were a fat, familiar armchair. A black cat is relating an interminable, maudlin epic on Janis's right. His story cranks on and on, bristling with details and turning on itself endlessly. To her left a silver-tongued Southern gentleman is peppering her by turns with come-ons and local history.

There's a pile of papers on the table with reviews of the concert. The local papers are ecstatic. The Louisville *Times* called it a "love feast," and the piece by the lady re-porter from the dressing room the night be-fore titled "Rock Queen Blasts Off Like an Apollo Rocket" launches into some pyro-technic journalism:

Like an Apollo rocket blasting off that's the power of Janis Joplin's voice. Howling, screeching, and penetrat-ing the air with such brilliance and force, you believe for a moment she could fill the Grand Canyon with sound.

That was amazing last night.

Dig it, that was only our fifth gig, we were just now getting our shit together. The band, for instance, had never seen me jump off the stage before. I do all kinds of stuff like that. They never see me say to the audience, "Pow, come on and stand up," right to those boys in the front row, and that's the country club boys going "Aaaaaghhh, aaaaaghhh."

That guy got up and really did it.

He grabbed my tits, that's the first thing he did. Once you get down on the floor and start dancing with them, unless they're sound asleep, that usually gets 'em up, because there's some kind of artificial barrier built into their minds between stage and us —that's the stage, that's the show. Once you break that barrier, and you jump down and walk out and touch them, and you say, "I'll dance with you, man, I'll get sweaty with you, come on, I'm with you, man, I just happen to be standing on stage"—once that barrier has been broken down, it just rocks right on out, man. It's fun, it's fun. I used to, and I still do, cause I got a beautiful home, and I'm sitting here in Louisville, Kentucky, it's raining, I'm in the bar, it's noon, I'm being treated rudely by four people out of five. Regular bar conversation, I love bar conversation, man—there's four people talking, nobody listening to anybody else, someone constantly offending, and a third person constantly apologizing. This third cat is saying, "I'm really sorry about a minute ago that I . . ." Talk about *cinéma vérité.* One thing I do not like is that star shit, man, I'm important so leave me alone, I'm saying, "I'm paying for my own drinks, so you can't bother me." That's what I say to those cats in the bars when they treat me funny and try to throw me out because my tits show and my feathers. It's all hippies, that's what I'm talking about, I'm not talking about getting treated like a pop star, because they don't even know that I'm a pop star, and they don't even relate to pop stars down here. What does a pop star mean to an 80-year-old bartender, a big flying fuck is what it means.

I went to a doctor the other day because one of the people in my office thinks I have a drinking problem, so I went to this doctor for special problems, and I told him, "I did this when I was 22, and I did this when I was 25, and I took this when I was 26, I started this at 14, I started this at 18, whatever they are, and I've been drinking a lot lately." He looked at me and said, "Man, I don't think you have a drinking problem, I think you're doing great." Most of my biggest problems now are what color scheme to use on my next string of beads.

That's the one thing I've learned about being on the road, that that music and that hour you get on stage is *all.* The rest of it's fucked up, full of shit, people trying to get something out of you, trying to talk to you, trying to sleep, you can't sleep, at two the bars are closed, it ain't really a rocking good time. The rocking good times you create, you bring the bottle yourself and go to someone else's room and say, "Let's rock." The road is just a hassle, the only thing you got out of it that's groovy is playing. Any musician that I see that's working, especially those six-day weeks, they're only doing it for their music, there's no other reason, no money is worth that grief, man. I have a beautiful home I could be at, playing with my dogs and getting my friends to visit me. I'd rather be there than here with a hangover trying to get myself together to go to a movie to cure absolute abject boredom in Louisville, Kentucky.

One of the Louisville reviews mentions Janis with Big Brother at Monterey.

"It's a very sad thing," Janis says soulfully. "I love those guys more than anybody else in the whole world, they know that. But if I had any serious ideas of myself as a musician, I had to leave. Getting off, real *feeling,* that's the whole thing of music for me. But by the end, we were shucking. We worked four, six nights a week for two years, doing the same tunes, and we'd put everything into them we could. We just used each other up."

I always thought Big Brother were really a great band.

Maybe I'll never find another one as good, but here's how I see the problem. I loved them, I still love them more than I love anyone else, and I'll never be as close to anyone in the world. James and Sam, those are the two men in my life. But there were all kinds of problems, like success came early, we never had a chance to rehearse any more, and when we did rehearse we never got any new material. We were on the road, we hit New York once, and bang! we were a big smash. We toured, toured, toured, a three-week rest in California, bang! hit the road again, no rehearsing. We're still doing "Combination of the Two," "Ball and Chain," we've been doing it for a year now, starting on the second year, "Combination of the Two," "Ball and Chain." As far as I'm concerned what drove me crazy was that I couldn't dredge up any sincerity in the music anymore. I mean it wasn't anybody's fault, it may be the fault that we got too much work, maybe it was the fault that everybody got too lazy, you know they thought, why work, man, which I think definitely is true. Finally I said to myself, listen, man, if you consider yourself a singer, you're an actor. I wanted to do some new shit, I had new ideas, maybe not concrete ones, but I had a feeling of the way I wanted to move, and I wasn't doing anything but standing still and being a success, so I quit. Maybe in a few years I'll have a different head, maybe I'll have developed that professional distance that says if it succeeds it's a

success, but at the time, and I still am, I started out in the world to be a beatnik, I wanted to do what felt right to me, I didn't want to be an executive or a teacher just because I could do it, I didn't want to be something just to make money, I wanted to be something because it felt right to me. I was very shaky at the beginning, everybody thought I was gonna go under. *Rolling Stone* said I was a failure, article coming out in *Playboy* next week says I was a failure, everyone says Janis lost it when she quit Big Brother, but I just won't quit, man. It's a real old article, way, way last year, when the San Francisco audience deserted me with my new group, they just turned their backs on me. Okay, we weren't as good as Santana, we'd only fucking been together two months, it will take a long while, I'm not a pro, I've only been with a bunch of friends. Now all of a sudden I'm faced with a pro group, trying to figure out material, arrange it, turn it into a product, and get the feeling right. I think we have the feeling right now, I want to learn now to stretch out a little bit, now it's still too crowded with Janis. But as soon as the guys get a little more confidence, I think we'll just stretch out a little more, just flow like it's supposed to. I ain't quitting, man, I won't quit for nobody, they'll have to throw me out if they want me to get out.

"There Must Be More to Love Than This"

THERE IS no show tonight, and the evening gapes ahead of us. There's a fantastic Country and Western show at the civic center: George Jones (from Beaumont, next door to

Janis's home town, Port Arthur), Tammy Wynette, and Jerry Lee Lewis. A moment's hesitation. Janis voices the paranoia: "You know what it's gonna be, dontcha? Ten thousand fuckin shitkickers going goony."

We resolve to go anyway, but late. Tammy Wynette is just about Janis's least favorite singer, so we miss the first half. To add to the surrealism of Janis in hillbilly heaven, the auditorium is right next door to some kind of penitentiary. Sloping up from backstage is a ramp with two guards cradling shotguns in their arms guarding a couple of open gratings.

Janis's credentials are not immediately recognized at the stage door. "Janis Joplin's the name," she says pointedly to the keeper of the gate. "I'm a singer—you *might* recognize my name." Eventually the emcee, a hearty Texan in a white ten-gallon hat ushers us in.

Inside, the scene is hard to believe. The crowd is close to 20,000, and initially it brings Janis down. "How come they didn't come see me 'n' then they come here to listen to all that old music?" she asks, a little naïvely. Every woman here looks like Tammy Wynette or Dolly Parton in a sculptured, glossy helmetlike hairdo that always looks tarty to Northern eyes. They're wearing little peeka-boo dresses that have a kind of rural innocence, as if they were still doing the Tennessee Waltz, and their dates, sleek as otters, slink back in their seats in Arnold Palmer golf sweaters and white Vent-Aire loafers.

We are allowed to stand behind the ramps. A conciliatory usher waves us back with Southern gentility. Janis manages to sneak by just the same. As chance would have it, the concert manager is the very same sergeant at arms who was in charge of keeping order at Janis's concert. He's on home ground now and he's about to take full advantage of it. "Listen," he says threatening in a bloated

fury, "I hay-ud enough of yew last ni-ut. Yew get the hail owt of ma sight!"

Meanwhile on stage Jerry Lee is getting into his big hit, "The Beer That Made Milwaukee Famous (Has Made a Loser Out of Me)." His slightest gesture sends the crowd into seething paroxysms. "You should be thanking your lucky stars they're not cannibals." Clark Pierson says grimly.

The taunting of the sergeant at arms eventually becomes too much for Janis and she crashes after him with the wobbling fury of a derailed train. "Tell me where to go, you asshole, and I'll go. Just leave me the fuck alone. Go on, you jerk-off, you're the mother fucker that stopped my show." He completely ignores her, and just as he is turning away to attend to something at the other end of the auditorium, Janis pulls out an empty bourbon bottle that she is about to crack him with. It takes the combined strength of Clark and me to pull her off.

Janis's attention soon turns to more immediate things. She's developed an almost frightening attraction for Jerry Lee's bass player, a 17-year-old hillbilly from Texas with long blond hair sleeked back like yellow sealskin.

"I must have that bow-ah," Janis says with contagious country inflection. "He is *one* bee-yute-ee-full boy."

By this time Jerry Lee is getting into his finale, snapping at the keys like a combine harvester. He kicks over his piano stool with contrived fury, but the gesture is so brutal that it stops you for a moment. The crowd is moaning and screaming. Waving his suggestive pinky, "Wiggle it around a little bit," is the equivalent of Moses parting the Dead Sea with his staff.

We go backstage with the emcee. Janis gets a better look at the bass player. And at close quarters she thinks he looks better than ever. Janis is pointing and making signs to him while he's on stage, and he just stares back in complete incomprehension.

"Is that your band out there?" Janis asks the emcee dumbly.

"No, ma'am, that's the band that travels with Jerry Lee."

"Do you happen to know the bass player in the group?" Janis asks innocently. "I mean, would you introduce me to him when the group comes off stage?"

"I'd be happy to, Jane-is," he says civilly, not realizing what's coming next.

"Can't wait to get my hands on that gorgeous-looking boy," Janis says.

"For you?" the emcee asks incredulously. "God, Jane-is, fer shame. Why, he wouldn't even know what to do with you."

"What he doesn't know how to do, honey," Janis says with a Mae West inflection, "I'll be glad to show him."

By this time Janis is hopping up and down on stage shouting "Play it, daddy, play it. Know something, man, that group is as tight as rope." As the bass player comes off stage Janis grabs him. "You're not climbing on a bus going somewhere tonight, are you honey?"

"Yes, I am, ma'am."

"No you're not, man, they told me you're not climbing on a bus, they told me you were all going to a party tonight," Janis shouts at him like an irate mother.

"I guess I didn't know about any of that," he says nervously.

"I thought we'd go back to the dressing room and get it on," Janis insists, but the kid just backs away apologetically.

"What's the matter, don't you like *sex?*" Janis shouts to him down the hallway.

"Well, yeah . . ." he says, fumbling for a doorknob. After he's gone, Janis asks rhetorically why none of the men she digs dig her. Clark philosophically offers an explanation: "Well, Janis, it could be your 'Glad to meet you, I'm yours' attitude."

"Breathless . . . Ah"

LINDA GAIL LEWIS takes us back to see her brother. His dressing room has the smoky, sweaty aura of a locker room with the guys sitting around chewing the fat. Janis is about as out of place here as Queen Victoria in Medicine Hat. "Hi ya, boys!" she hollers tinkling into the room. "Hey man, I saw a movie of you yesterday, the Toronto Festival. Man, you were really cookin.' "

Jerry Lee is sitting with no shirt on astride a bench surrounded by local deejays, buddies, and members of his group, mostly older ruddy-faced Southern gentlemen who all looked like they were brought up on a diet of Jimmy Rodgers and mustard greens. "It would be really better for your voice if you wrapped a towel around your throat," Janis says solicitously.

"Don't bother *me* none," Jerry Lee says breathlessly.

"Would you like a *drink,* then?" Janis asks.

"I could go for a good strong one," Jerry Lee says.

"There ain't stronger than what I got, man, Southern Comfort."

"Yeah, I reckon that stuff is about 100 proof," Jerry Lee says testily.

"I do the best I can, what do you think I drink it for, boredom? These boys don't know how to take me, man. Guess I'll just have to learn how to leave."

Janis is hip that this isn't exactly her scene, but she digs it. And she's so macho that she's knocking over old Jerry Lee. Janis is not exactly Jerry Lee's scene either. He just doesn't know what to do with her, for a start, and he sure isn't going to compete. He's too subtle and sardonic for that. He sort of tailgates along as Janis boomerangs around the room. He looks at her searchingly with a sarcastic tilt of his head, as if she were a ballsy materialization of Yma Sumac. What would he have done with Ma Rainey either, for that matter?

"On a record of yours you've got a song by a silver-tongued devil by the name of Kris Kristofferson?" Janis asks, awkwardly trying to start a conversation.

Jerry Lee: "That boy can sure drink wine, I can tell you."

"Not only wine, man, that cat can outdrink me in tequila, and I thought I could cover that on anyone. He was at my house three weeks, couldn't leave."

"Him and . . . Silverstein . . ." Jerry Lee says, fumbling the pass. Didn't he write 'Once More With Feeling'?"

"Right, man, he kept playing that every morning soon as he got up," Janis cackles.

Jerry Lee can be very ornery. He isn't your typical country bumpkin, not by half a yard. No, sir, this boy is *sharp*. You just have to hear the way he sings "She Only Woke Me Up to Say Goodbye" to know what brand of goods Jerry Lee has in his store. Jerry Lee: "He wrote a real good song that I was gonna record one time, number one song it would have been. Anyway, I was drivin' and I heard this show on the radio, you know, one of those talk, interview type programs, and all he could talk about was Johnny Cash, Johnny Cash, Johnny Cash. When I got back I sent him this letter, said 'Why don't you send it to Johnny Reb?' "

"How was your concert last night?" Jerry Lee asks, trying to get off the subject of Kristofferson.

"We had a bony-fide, all-in, full-tilt freak-out last night, and then they tried to stop it."

"Was it a *riot?*" Jerry Lee asks sardonically.

"No, man, they just wanted to dance. Hey, it was at Freedom Hall, get it?" Janis asks.

"They were beatin my people on the head, man, and I just said 'out!' "

"Things *can* get out of hand," Jerry Lee says, palming it off.

"There ain't no such thing as outa hand, man. If the cops leave them alone there wouldn't be any trouble in the first place."

"Maybe they get wild because of you, Janis," Linda Gail suggests.

"Can't help it, man, been this way for ten years, my mother threw me out of the house when I was 14."

Combination of the Two

JANIS WAS BORN on January 19, 1943, under the sign of Capricorn. She was only mildly attached to the paraphernalia of astrology and psychedelia, although she did recognize in herself afflictions of that sign—intense introspection and the tendency to go from the heights of ecstasy to the depths of depression, the goat on the peak, the fish in the deep.

If she had been named for the two-faced god of this month, Janus, god of gates and transitions, one face toward the past, the other toward the future, the choice could hardly have been more appropriate. She lived in pain, exposed as she was to the embryonic paradoxes of her inner conflicts.

Janis's publicist, Myra Friedman, even saw an almost total split between the image by which she was best known and her personal aspirations. "The image she sometimes cultivated and sometimes had forced upon her, that of the 'get it while you can girl,' she said, was not accurate:

"I think Janis knew that wasn't really where she was at. Maybe a part of her believed that, but I think the most honest part didn't. She wasn't a conservative girl—that's ridiculous—but she had a lot of needs that were just like everyone else's. She was accepting of a lot of different kinds of people.

"Recently I met her at the Chelsea Hotel —she always stayed there when she was in New York—and she had been reading a book. It was *Look Homeward Angel.* She told me she read a lot, but 'Don't tell anybody.'

Sam Gordon, who ran Janis's music-publishing firm, recalled going to a pub recently for a drink with her.

"We were rapping about what we wanted from life," he told me. "I said I wished I was on the road again instead of in my comfortable suburban life I've been living for a while now."

" 'I'll take a split-level bungalow with two kids any day,' she said. I asked if that was what she really wanted and she said, 'Yeah, that's what I really want.' "

This lesion of identity threatened to undermine everything Janis did. Perhaps this is the enigma presented to everyone who tries to scale the heights. The wall of Paradise, which conceals God from man, is said to be constituted of coincidence of opposites, its gate guarded by "the highest spirit of reason, who bars the way until he has been overcome," Nicholas of Cusa wrote in *De Visione Dei.*

Pairs of opposites, which seem to have been more profuse in Janis than in most, are the crashing rocks that crush the traveler, but through which the aspirant must pass.

For Janis the rocks were the two spheres of her brain. Within there was always conflict. The sensual child straining at the leash, filled with poignant fears and delights, yearning for impossibly beautiful romantic meetings, night sounds, perfume of wild flowers, trodden brutally by her *wraith,* a double-walker of ominous suggestion, doubting, nagging, a self-destructive embryonic parent, present at every wish. Spiked with anguish and remorse, which fear and jealousy employ to bind them to their objects of attraction, this darker side was a seering eye whose orbit unravels all illusions. Between these two grinding globes Janis crouched at the Hippocampal gate with her only two defenses, smack and Time.

In "Try" Janis sang "If it's a dream I don't want nobody to wake me" and only in dreams are such opposing contradictions as plagued Janis resolved. To lean too heavily on their fragile fabric is to impose the machinery of fantasy on unyielding matter. Fitzgerald had seen the same fatal flaw in Zelda, believing in the impossible, and then attempting to set it in motion: "Her dominant idea and goal is freedom without responsibility, which is like gold without metal, spring without winter, youth without age, one of those maddening coo-coo mirages." (*The Crack-Up*)

So I said, "Hon, I want the sunshine"
Yeah take the stars out of the night.
[Spoken] Hey, come on and give it to me, babe
Cause I want it right now!

            Janis Joplin, "Turtle Blues"

The exceptions, naturally, have a very unhappy childhood and youth; for to be essentially reflective at an age which is naturally immediate, is the depths of melancholy. But they are rewarded; for most people do not succeed in becoming spirit, and all the fortunate years of their immediateness are, where spirit is concerned, a loss, and therefore they never attain to spirit. But the unhappy childhood and youth of the exception is transfigured into spirit.

        —Kierkegaard, *Journals,* 1848

"I was a sensitive child," Janis recalled, "I had a lot of hurts and confusions. You know, it's hard when you're a kid to be different, you're full of things, and you don't know what it's about."

And there were many who, unknown to Janis, were also going through the same thing. In fact, in one way or another, everyone who ever listened with sympathetic ear to her records or identified with her galactic stage presence had gone through some of that pain. Her songs were just what she did with her pain.

The psychoanalyst Marie Bonaparte expressed the magical climate of childhood like this: "The days of the child seem to unfold in some sense outside of our time. These days of childhood—let us each recall them—seem to the child as if they were eternal."

If Janis contributed anything at all to our culture, our freedoms even, it was this image of the gigantic child, absorbed in play, willing to let go the monster of self if only it would let *her* go.

Her unhappy childhood and her limitless sadness precipitated in her a hidden inwardness, and a personal life detached from her roots, an effect that in other, more religious times would have been called simply "spirit."

My Daddy Stood All the Way and Cried

Genius is the ability to put into effect what is your mind. There is no other definition of it.
—F. Scott Fitzgerald, *The Crack-Up*

THERE MUST have come a point when Janis came face to face with her constellated demons. One night, when no distractions filled the void, its breath must have impregnated her just as God is said to have put the stars in the firmament, "all the host of them by the breath of His mouth." And, like the insidious water grandfather of Russian folktales, with his spectral talent for coaxing into his toils unhappy young women who like to dance on moonlit nights, the demon must have seduced her in the sweet darkness.

Her parents could tell. And they were dis-

tressed and hurt as any parents would be to find that, in spite of all their precautions, their child had been infested with incubi. Her mother's rage was not even contained by her death. She could never accept what Janis had "made of herself."

Janis grew up during the 50's, the adolescence of a new America, violent, pimply, naïve, stoked with uncontrollable energies that it did not know how to handle. This ambivalent time, half angry and wounded and half complacent, was a last time of innocence for America before James Dean smashed through the windscreen of its past and brought on the perpetual teen dream that was to fatally undermine the old cohesive establishment of Eisenhower, "that piece of chewing gum rolling around the jaws of history." Janis was like a capsule of all that undetonated energy forced in on itself, as if the decade had condensed in her, Little Queenie jumping up on stage and kissing the future.

Janis created her own style, aside from her clothes ("clothing as clowning"), which exposed their own defiance and sexual liberation. It was her *hair,* "positively triangular in its electricity," as Lillian Roxon described it, and with her compassionate insight caught her truth beautifully: "I read with some sorrow, in *Time* magazine, I think it was, that someone said that before it all happened, the success and everything, Janis was a pig. But beauty had a way of flowing out again, so I guess there were as many times when she looked truly homely as there were times when she looked truly beautiful. And that went for a lot of her sisters. I think she taught America that beauty didn't *have* to be a constant, it could ebb and flow and surprise you by being there one minute and not the next."

Hair is not just an outward sign like clothes, but literally the outgrowth of the inward, the sexually loaded seed pod flowering from the roots of the head. The emergence of hair as a presence is the expression of the almost intangibly archaic idea "that the head contains a different factor, the procreative life, soul or spirit that survives after death, and the seeds of a new life," says Onians in *Origins of European Consciousness.*

Jimi Hendrix, in his own intuitive way, had made the connection: "Fuzzy hair is radiant. My hair is electric, man, it picks up *all* the vibrations."

Janis had the first electric larynx. Her cry of love was in her voice, just as Jimi's was in his "ax." It was filled with all the cackling, shrieking, fuzzing, whining feedback of the electric guitar. Unconsciously it imitated the guitar as totally as jazz singers of an earlier age had imitated through their scatting the reedy sounds of trumpets, saxes, and trombones. She was the first "cordless woman," which is perhaps why she was always so restless, all that static building up every day and screaming out at her concerts like a 50-amp fuse about to blow.

"Oh, Lawdy, Those Dogs of Mine— They Sure Do Worry Me All the Time"

"ALL TRUTHS lie waiting in all things," wrote Whitman. "They unfold themselves more fragrant than . . . roses from living buds, whenever you fetch the spring sunshine moistened with summer rain. But it must be in yourself. It shall come from your soul. It shall be love."

We become what we wish for. Consummations draw us out. To fulfill them completely

is often fatal. Janis perhaps listened too closely to inner voices pulling her down, beckoning her to withdraw from her family and friends, into the goblin market. The journey from the external to the internal is accomplished with the aid of all the secret helpers of our nursery. But it is by retreating from the world of secondary effects, secret relations with the demonic, that the initiation can be effected. It is only in these *causal zones,* when one has broken through to the undistorted direct experience, that the real difficulty of the world can be known.

"I'm a victim of my own insides," Janis said. "There was a time when I wanted to know everything. I read a lot. I guess you'd say I was pretty intellectual. It's odd. I can't remember when it changed. It used to make me very unhappy, all that feeling. I just didn't know what to do with it, but now I've learned how to make feeling work *for* me. I'm full of emotion, and I want a release. And if you're on stage and if it's really working and you've got the audience with you, it's a *oneness* you feel. I'm into me, plus they're into me, and everything comes together. You're full of it. I don't know. I just want to feel as much as I can. It's not wise always, but it's super-valid, and maybe it's much wiser. It's what 'soul' is all about.

"I was in Port Arthur, and we used to listen to a lot of jazz, and one day I was in a record store and I found a record by Odetta, and I bought it, and I really dug it, and I played it at a bunch of parties, and everyone liked it. This friend of mine told me about somebody he heard of called Leadbelly, he bought Leadbelly records, which were even better, far-out country blues. Odetta was singing oxdriver songs. Anyway, we used to go to parties and play records and talk about poetry, and one day we were out at this lifeguard tower, we used to go to all the beaches and stay for the night, just sit on the beach and talk and drink beer, and we'd go to this old coast guard shack, a little tiny building, you'd go all the way to the top, it was a room with four walls, all glass, and you'd look out on all this water and marsh and we used to sit up there with a candle and a bottle of Jim Beam and a couple of Cokes and sit around and talk. We were up there one day and someone said, 'I wish we had a record player,' and I said, 'I can sing.'

" 'Come on, Janis, cut it out.'

"I said, 'I can, too, man,' they said, 'Come on,' so I started singing a real Odetta . . . [sings really loud] Ya-la-la . . . I came out with this huge voice.

"They said, 'Far out, Janis, you're a *singer!*'

"I said, 'No I'm not, man, fuck off, man.'

"They told me I had a good voice, and I thought, Wow, that's far out, and when I played records, I'd sing them to myself.

"When I'm there, I'm not here," Janis said later. "I can't talk about my singing; I'm inside it. How can you describe something you're inside of?"

PART THREE

THE CATTERPILLER ON THE LEAF

"The only true wisdom," the caribou wizard Igjugarjuk told the explorer Rasmussen, "lives far from mankind, out in the great loneliness, and it can be reached only through suffering. Privation and suffering alone can open the mind of man to all that is hidden to others."

—H. Osterman,
Report of the Fifth Thule Expedition, 1921–24

THE CATTERPILLER ON THE LEAF

The Martyred Slaves to Time

WE LAND IN New York on a drizzling late afternoon. Outside the terminal we are balancing moments, waiting for the limos to arrive, as the afternoon stares back at us under an impacted dark gray cumulus. The atmosphere has the metallic odor of a recently vacated motel room, and the air is disturbed and buzzing with the thick hum of the city in the distance, murmuring abrasions of things turned on.

Underneath the huge cement arches of the arrivals building the girl who reminds Janis of herself is standing. "Hey, man," Janis says in her disappointed voice, "aren't any of those guys going to pick up on her? That's me, man, sittin right there, ten years ago when I was bummin around hitchhikin here and there, hoping some cat would come along and take me off . . . or someone would at least feel sorry for me, let me fall out on their floor. She'll probably have to go through the same shit I went through before she gets herself together. Hey, man, *I'd* pick up on her . . ."

The temptation to tamper with time is almost irresistible for Janis as she watches the shy defiant movements of this young girl with crinkly yellow hair reading some heavy paperback, *searching,* longing, afraid and filled with all the voluptuous wishing in the world. . . .

You can see the thought running back and forth in her mind, seeking herself through all the empty rooms and street corners of her past as if she could just slip back and help herself get around some bad *miscalculations.*

Finally John Fisher (of Love Limos) arrives. Janis is always glad to see him, someone she's always at ease with. He is a good sign, all dressed in black as he moves with demonic agility about the car.

After checking into the hotel we go out to look for somewhere to talk. There's a restaurant in the hotel. It is one of those incredible romantic fabrications that are a sanctuary for women of a certain age, involving pristine trellis fences trailing with garlands of artificial flowers, a watercolor by Cecil Beaton of the Immaculate Conception of High Tea, intended to give the perpetual illusion of an untroubled afternoon late in the summer of 1926. The congregation is uniformly tucked into little wrought-iron tables. Janis clanks into this Ballet Russe rococo like Genghis Khan at the court of Vienna. The room turns toward us in a haunted gaze. Janis, out of perversity, wants to stay; then, realizing it is going to be a performance, and the audience not exactly appreciative, we split. Nobody's was Janis's nest, and that was her next thought. Myra rejects that as too distracting. "Whaddya mean *distracting?* What you mean is there's too damn much *talent* there!"

We decide on the Cedar Bar as neutral ground. It used to be a hangout of the abstract expressionists. Willem de Kooning is supposed to have knocked someone's tooth out here, or something like that. Anyway, in those days it was only a seedy bar; now it's just a very pleasant reconstruction. There's a sprinkling of demure hippies, but most of the men look like they had been to school with Holden Caulfield.

"This place looks as square as hell," Janis declares, "but after a few drinks I guess it don't make much difference where you are. Am I right?"

There are some for whom the night holds no terrors; on the contrary, for them it is the day with its hordes of *martyred slaves to Time* that is haunted. And of all these night figures—criminals, insomniacs, whores, alcoholics, the inconsolable, the dreamers and lovers—Janis was Queen. At home in bars as anywhere, she always looked better as the evening progressed, like a night-blooming flower. The light of the day scanned her too cruelly as if it peevishly resented her preference for the night. And she *dressed* for night in the outrageous costumes of circus performers—belly dancers, and opera singers— like black Southern *girls who paint themselves bright as savages to stand out against the tropical summer.* It was only in *daylight* that she looked absurd. "With all those bells and junk tied around her," someone once unkindly said about Janis, whom they'd seen banging on the door of a bar in the early afternoon, "I thought at first that she was some college girl pledging a sorority." It was the kind of remark that could have been made only by someone who had never accompanied Janis on her long fantastic night journeys where these phosphorescent costumes became her robes of office, as she brazenly sunned herself in artificial light, a true child of the moon and its incandescent offspring. The night drew out the best in her, as hidden currents, pushed and pulled by

lunar correspondence, washed up little treasures with her tides.

The evening flows on, and raucous voices, noises of conspiratorial complaint, brutal shrieks of transformation, and intimate sighs echo around the room like horns on a still night at sea. As we descend, sealed off in our private worlds (imaginary bathyspheres), the bar filled with memories, we take flight on scents and sounds, and peer out nostalgically at places and forms swimming by, as close as breath on a pane and as remote, letting past moments rub suggestively against the glass.

Is This Person That's Talking Me?

I THINK it's time to order a few drinks at a time . . . [Janis says]. I feel better now, I was feeling really bogged down on the plane. I was talking with this doctor last week and he told me there is a pharmacology to alcohol. There are certain chemical reactions in your body that create energy here, exhaust there . . .

I heard it's related to morphine . . .

Oh, no! He didn't tell me that. What he told me was—I ordered an Irish coffee and he said, That's a Dexamyl. He said that chemically and molecularly and in the enzyme reactions and the whole medical shot that it was a kissing cousin to Dexedrine in the way it reacted on your whole body. It's the same drug, and alcohol was almost the same as Miltown.

Just changing states.

Yeah, I get tired of being in the same place. I hate boredom. I hate boredom more than anything. I'd rather be a junkie than be bored, and being a junkie is just about the most boring place to be.

That was a strange town, Louisville.

Yeah, that was far out. I haven't had a confrontation like that in years, like on the street. Usually, when I walk down the street there's four or five of them looking at me, but there was a *crowd*—sixty or more kids across the street coming up and talking, asking questions.

That was beautiful . . .

They always are, man. I mean, you can't put down somebody for loving you. I don't think there's any performer who is that much of an egomaniac that they don't need those people; no one is, baby, no one . . . [*Someone plays "Down On Me" on the jukebox.*] First song I ever learnt. I'm getting tired of singing it. They made me change the words when I went into the studio.

Why?

Because they were all about God and shit, so I had to talk about "believe in your brother, have faith in man." Same idea but not so gospel. [*"Call On Me" is playing on the jukebox.*] This one Sam [Andrew] wrote. He wrote some great songs—"Bye Bye Baby"— great songs, but every time we played 'em we fucked 'em up. So we stopped playing them. We started playing the easy ones, fast ones.

How did you get into singing blues?

When I first started singing I was copping Bessie Smith records. I used to sing exactly like Bessie Smith, and when I started singing with Big Brother that was the only thing I knew how to do, and used to wonder—especially when people would clap and tell me I was good—I used to wonder, "Is that real, or is that something I've learned to do with my voice?" But I think after doing it for a few years I got to understand that it all ties in. I

used to ask guys I was balling "Do I ball like I sing? Is it really me?" That's what I'm trying to say. It is really me, or am I putting on a show . . . and that's what I wonder sometimes when I'm talking. Is this person that's talking me? Does what I am saying correlate with my music?

Oh, yeah, of course it does.

I think so, too. I actually think it's all me.

Well, it's like in Kansas City, the second show especially, what you are doing is taking people from one level and lifting them up . . .

And insisting on it!

What happens, I mean do you know the point where it turns around?

Yeah, I know exactly what happens, man. I was on stage, and I looked out, and I knew they weren't ready. We were doing "Piece of My Heart"—you know you can do a lot of different things, you know sometimes they get up spontaneously. Out in the Midwest, they don't. They aren't supposed to stand up, and they know it. It's hard to get 'em up. But, I remember I was singing "Piece of My Heart," you know that "Come on, come on" line—well, you know the guitar solo that leads into that part? I came in early, and I walked all the way to the front of the stage and shouted [*in a hoarse whisper*], "Come on, come on!" and just fucking stamping my foot and saying "I'm not going to sing anymore unless you do something," you know, and they're going "Whoo—ooo—ooo, yes, mam! Yes, mam, yes, mam!" A riot. Groovy. All they want is a little kick in the ass. You know, sometimes I jump off the stage and grab somebody and say, "Let's dance." When they reach a certain level, you know they want to be lifted but they're scared. Then all you gotta do is give the old kick in the ass, a big fucking kick in the ass, man.

Then the promoters get goony, turn the lights on, pull the power, but by then it's all over [*cackles*]. I dig it! I dig it so much, man! Cause I figure it this way, man, those kids living in the Midwest, like I was raised in Texas, man, and I was an artist, and I had all these ideas and feelings that I'd pick up in books, and my father would talk to me about it, and I'd make up poems and things. And, man, I was the only one I'd ever met. There weren't any others. There just wasn't *anybody*, man, in Port Arthur. There were a couple of old ladies who used to do water-colors and paint still lives, and that was it. And I'd look at these books of paintings and go "Wow!" and I'd try and paint that free, to let it go. I mean, in other words, in the Midwest you got no one to learn from because there's not a reader down the street you can sneak off and talk to. There's nobody there. Nobody. I remember when I read that in *Time* magazine about Jack Kerouac —otherwise I'd've never known—I said "Wow!" and split. Kids from the Midwest, their whole fucking thing is to sit in 247 and be still, "I'll give you until eleven o'clock, and that's it." They get "Do this, do that!" It's never occurred to them that they could *not* go in the army. They were told to go in the army. You know, it's a thing I do—not in defiance, it's a side trip—you know, I figure if you can take an audience that have been told what to do all their lives and they're too young or too scared or whatever—I wasn't scared, but, you know, most of the kids brought up in that scene are. You know, "Daddy wouldn't like it." Or the South, or hey, man, California, but it's worse there, because California or New York, there are freaks all over, and they know there are other ways of life. The point being that out there they do not know there is another way of life. They've never seen a freak, and if they have they probably just think they're dope addicts, fuck-ups and horrible degener-

ate uglies. If you can get them once, man, get them standing up when they should be sitting down, sweaty when they should be decorous, smile when they should be applauding politely, and I think you sort of switch on their brain, man, so that makes them say: "Wait a minute, maybe I can do anything." Whoooooo! It's life. That's what rock 'n' roll is for, turn that switch on, and man, it can all be. I hate to tell you that it can, but it could be, and you're a fool not to try. I mean you may not end up happy, but I'm fucked if I'm not going to try. That's like committing suicide the day you're born if you don't try.

When you're on the road it must be hard to make it happen all the time. Do you rely on things to get you going?

You mean tricks, gimmicks? Sure, I got a thing, I can't talk about it, but you have all kinds of tricks that I put at the beginning of the first tune to turn me on.

Like what kind of things?

Movement things, like the way you move, a certain instrument you listen to, I watch my equipment men, they know me real good, and they love me, so like if I'm feeling scared . . . if you aren't always on, man, then you damn sure better get on. I don't care how fuckin tired you are, so I suppose in one way it is somewhat insincere. Like Mike Bloomfield, he only plays when he feels like it, well, that's fine, man, he's a very lucky guy. I've walked on stage bored shitless, on a bummer and everything, and walked off goony, so I don't think you can wait till you feel like playing. Sometimes playing is the only way you got out. . . . Sure there is an element of acting. The biggest thing to me is—I don't know about the element of acting . . . I've been talking to Michael Pollard about acting, and I don't know whether I can act or not, but I can act like *me*. I can act like me like a son of a bitch. The most important thing to my performance is to kick me off, the more I find, the more I use.

That's the amazing thing about a great performance, that it can be very real and very structured at the same time.

Sure it's structured. Cause I remember when I was playing with Big Brother sometimes I'd get so excited I'd stop singing and start jumping up and down. I don't do that any more because I know when it reaches a certain point, it's got to go here, and you gotta do it. Playing music isn't just letting it all hang out, that's like shitting, that's letting it all hang out, too. Playing is like taking a feeling and like turning it into a finished, tight thing that is readable and understandable to the people who are looking at it. It's not just for you, you can't just sing how *you* feel, you've got to take how you feel, sift it through whatever vocal chords you have, whatever instrumentation you have, whatever arrangements you have, and try and create a swelling feeling in an audience.

Morning and Evening of the First Day

I HAD SEEN Janis performing in Panhandle Park and I had seen her at Monterey, but I remember her most vividly at the Summer Solstice in San Francisco in 1967. She was standing in front of this elongated Forties airport car smoking a cigar and drinking out of a bottle. Among all the fantastic images that arise from that day—sorcerers juggling red faces, gypsies, yage giants and self-anointed princes, clowns and Harlequins from the mime troupe pirouetting on the lawn, monks, and hordes of smoldering Angels, children, naked as Adam on the first day of creation, clutching balloons on the edge of a rain forest, Indians and wagonmasters, and all the flyers, walkers and divers that could be assembled in one place at one time—Janis seemed still the *most* fantastic and the most real. Perhaps it was just that among all the impersonations in the park that afternoon her emanation seemed the most plausible. It became her and she became it.

Within all this insanity, a motorcycle cop, his boot on the running board, is writing out a ticket in all seriousness for "an illegally parked vehicle in a public place." As Janis catches sight of him, she taps her cigar and gingerly moves around the curves of the old limousine with the deliberate trajectory of a planet, swaying in that articulated gait that always made W. C. Fields look like he was trying to stand upright in a small rowboat.

I remember asking her if I could take a photograph of her with Big Brother. "To tell ya the truth, honey, I don't know where the boys went to," she says in her croaky little-girl voice, her face as serious as an old plate. I am amazed, but I notice uneasily that the fantasy is a resassurance. The image recedes rapidly, telescoping to a small round disk of light as if it had been sucked back into the vacuum of time, and all that is left is Janis's shitkicking grin floating across the zero blue sky of the afternoon like the smoky trace of a Cheshire cat.

The day had begun with little altars of twigs and grass at dawn on Mount Tamalpais, offerings to the local deities, the axis of smoke ascending from the hub of the earth to the celestial wheel. It is the festival of the center of the year, symbolized by the forefinger and "U," the erotic vowel, heather and wild bees. The goddess of this solstice is a queen bee about whom male drones swarm in midsummer, and recollections of this day seem to hover around Janis, just as bees will hum over invisible tables where they once sipped honey. Janis did then, most of all, embody the spirit of midsummer: sensual, ripe, fiery and dancing barefoot; like a young Kaffir girl delirious with pleasure, she moves rhythmically to the accompaniment of her own daydreams, scarcely less amazing than the image of the Triple Goddess herself that Jonathan Swift collected at Lough Crew: "an ancient, ageless childlike giantess, her car drawn by sparks of light who hunts the white mountain deer with seventy hounds that have the names of birds."

Everywhere bubbling powers of unknown valence are breaking into play—Hendrix clambering up onto the back of Big Brother's sound truck to shoot some double exposures with his Instamatic camera, an agile, numinous figure mischievously alighting on the earth: "I long to be a shimmering silver light on the screen."

Loops of meaning curl in cool blades of grass: the dream of a foot with eyes set in the instep; polished stones tumbling out of heaven; *Eternity in an Hour;* vanishing outlines, kerfs and cusps . . . the snake draws a circle round the dreamer blending all these plaintive singing reflections of the chromatic eye of God with the actual joys of the afternoon: teams of shouting, screaming, dancing children swimming in the wake of the sound trucks. Janis is on the bed ladling out her raunchy blues like nursery rhymes to little groups of awestruck kids who stare vacantly at this mirage from the dusty area in front of the truck. A figure leans over the edge of the truck, grinning like a hookah, his features distorted by the astigmatic focus of memory so that the tip of his nose is all that remains of reality. He is passing out handfuls of joints. Someone says they've been rolled from grass they planted on that spot earlier in the year. As the image of Janis and Big Brother singing from the platform of their truck surrounded by her band of followers begins to oscillate and decompose, I hurriedly fixed in my mind its photomorphic de-

tails in R. Crumb's bold pneumatic outlines, where hopefully it will linger a few moments longer.

In spite of subsequent contractions, and despite its pantomime of mysteries, that morning and afternoon will always seem magically suspended, as if somehow removed from the onward rush of things and events, and at the center of this warp of time is Janis, radiant, earthy, vulnerable as the moments that went to make it up, and yet, because of personal demons who would not let her rest, forcing her to trace out a vaster plan, she is fixed in time and space by the coordinates of the mind's eye as firmly as a point in the celestial sphere.

As the revelers, weary from wonders, like interplanetary visitors tired from their first day exploring the earthly paradise, stumble, dance (the bands still playing) and blow themselves into the sea at the edge of Golden Gate Park, and as the great sun wobbling on the edge of extinction showers everything with flakes of rusty light, it seemed for an instant that the original state of mankind must have resembled this day in its infinite possibilities, and that Janis, naïve, filled with wonder and surprise, may have been its first beautiful child.

One of the first times I saw you was at the Summer Solstice. All the groups on back of the trucks really blew everyone's minds.

Yeah, we walked over to Haight Street and bought some wine, me and Sunshine and our dog George. We walked, sauntered, *sashayed* to Haight Street and bought some more wine, that's all I remember. I think I met Freewheelin' Frank that day, too.

His book really blew my mind.

Well, some of them are real good friends of mine, Sweet William, Crazy Pete. Freewheelin' I met a long time ago. Moose is a good friend. I don't really know too many others, as evidenced in the fact that I got punched out by a bunch of them at a dance I played for them. The trouble with them for me is that . . . see, as friends, they are just people . . . but the club itself I think is inconsiderate. What I mean to say is, like after I got slugged the guy came up and said, "Ya shoulda tole me who ya wuz." You should be consistent! Be shitty all the time, then you can be a genuine outlaw and be proud of yourself. My quarrel with the Angels is just that my chemistry works at a different rate.

When did you first come to San Francisco?

I first came in '62. I used to hang out in North Beach. I used to sing at the Coffee Confusion, sang there a couple of times. Sang at the hootenanies for beer. After I sang I got one beer. It was the tail end of the beatnik era. There were still tourists coming around; it was an excuse to hang out on the street for spare change and some wine. I got beat up a couple of times. See this scar? Big lump from getting beat up by four spades; I'll never take a good picture. Then I came back and joined Big Brother. That was one beautiful time, man. They weren't professional musicians, they were all friends, just people. We used to walk down Haight Street drinking Ripple. Now Haight Street is so weird. Remember that *Suddenly Last Summer* movie where that guy gets eaten by cannibals? Well, that almost happened to me the last time I was there. I got out of my car. "It's Janis Joplin, it's Janis Joplin. Hey, give me this, give me that . . ." pushing, pulling on me, trying to aggravate me. It didn't used to be like that. I used to hang out in the park and have a good time. I wish it were that way now, but you can't go home again. We played at the Avalon because we were Chet's group. First time I went to the Fillmore we weren't with Chet by then. He was running the Avalon, and we didn't feel he could handle us *and* do that at the same

time. It was some kind of benefit on a Sunday night. Bill Graham sees us coming up the stairs, and he threw us out. I said, "Why are you doing that, man, we're not with Chet any more." He said, "Because you aren't any damn good." Oh, he likes us now. He's good to any group that's made it.

Tell me about Big Brother, I mean the people in the group.

Well, let's see, Dave I'd say is the solidest guy in that group. He was an art teacher before. You could always rely on him in a kind of karma way. Peter is more crazy than he thinks he is; he thinks he is very middle class and he just went a little goony, but he is really goony, man, that's how goony he is.

He wrote . . .

Yeah, "Caterpillar" for example. If that's not madness, what is? "I'm a pteradactyl for your love." And James, beautiful, strong man. He never had any of that Indian bullshit, but he *had* an ethereal quality . . . all good soul. I loved him so. We have a little love affair, almost broke up our band. And Sam is like, you know, a very intelligent cat, you wouldn't know it because he's so good-looking. . . . One day I was on a plane, walking down the aisle, and you know, everybody's reading *Newsweek* and stuff, the Kansas City *Star* and stuff, and Sam's reading a book in Latin! But I think Sam is a little thwarted in his music thing. I don't know why but I don't think he's found the right way for his music thing to come out of him, yet. We were very close in a communal type thing, me and Big Brother. It was great to be playing again with them at the Avalon. It was such a gas, because I'd been on the road with a second group, and it just got worse and worse, and we weren't gettin along, and the music wasn't together, and we had to finish the tour. . . . Sometimes music isn't quite a *joy,* and it wasn't with the last group . . . like Blind Faith, those guys didn't dig playing together, so anyway, one day I had some little time off, and I heard Big Brother were playing at the Family Dog, and I went over, and they asked me to come up, and I was so jacked that they asked me, and we hugged and kissed, and then . . . they didn't remember any of our old songs, and we had to make up one. They didn't even remember "Piece of My Heart." I was really crushed. So word got around and Bill Graham decided to capitalize on it. He needed a name, and Janis was the name, so he got us together again for one night. It was really just like a family reunion, man. It was so much fun, sittin on the floor, drinkin tequila, kissin and talkin about old times. I remember walkin on stage and saying, "It's so nice to play with friends . . . my people, man." But you can't go home again, you can't go back, right? I have learned from experience, and my experience is in my music and in my personality, and they have changed. It's like ex-lovers who don't ball any more—we'd drive each other crazy. I know I can count on them. If I get busted, I know I can count on them to bail me out . . . I know when James got into trouble, I was there . . . it really was a horrible, traumatic thing for him.

I guess the most upset people ever got was when you split with Big Brother.

They sure laid a lot of shit on me.

The second group had a little bit of that Motown lineup, you know, with a lead singer and an anonymous backup group.

I didn't mean it to go that far. To that degree. I wanted them to be a group, but it never jelled. This group I have now already does. I can't work with a backup band either, I need the emotion from the band. But I don't think it's possible to be on a San Francisco free thing with me and the band *totally*

because I'm in front, I'm in the spotlight, and if something goes wrong I'm the one who has to carry it.

Why was Sam the only member of Big Brother that you took with you when you formed your second band?

Because Sam and I sang very well together and wrote very well together, and I thought we would really do well together, but we didn't get it on. Now, John [Till] is what I consider a great guitarist for me. Shit, baby, he's playing a lot of stuff back there, you don't even notice. Like tunes we have to do like "Maybe," for example, you know that's got a dominant horn line. When the organist is playing the line, the organ is such a muted instrument that it really isn't carrying it. John's playing the trumpet part plus the tink-tink-tink-tink guitar part plus the pows when I want 'em plus the fills, and the booms and the bangs, and the chicks, and the ting-ting players and the bong-bong players . . . I watch him during rehearsal and he has to play lead plus he has to play the pattern. I guess all guitar players have to do that. I guess I never noticed before, because I had two guitar players.

"One Good Man," you wrote that, right?

Yeah, it's a blues. Blues are easy to write. Just a lonely woman's song. Lookin for one good man. And I've been lookin. It's an eternal blues. About me trying to act tough, and nobody noticed I wasn't. It's like "Turtle Blues."

Who wrote "Light Is Faster Than Sound?"

Peter, Peter Albin. I wrote the "whooo, whooo, whooo" part though. See, with Big Brother it was usually a collective effort, except for Sam's songs. Like "Call On Me," "Combination of the Two," for example. They really sounded like that when he came in with them, but Peter's songs, and songs like that, we would start with an idea, play it, until it took form. Like "Ball and Chain" when it started didn't have that much silence and drama, it's just that we played it so many times and knew it so well we learned to capitalize on it. One beat rather than four medium beats. It was, dare I say it? [*in a voice*] an organic product. It's a lot easier to get your shit together, you know, at the Matrix, at the Avalon. You can fuck off there, you can be good, bad, great there, in front of your friends and it's all just fun. After Monterey, and after New York, I don't feel that way anymore. It's important how I sound now, it's not just for fun anymore, although I do it for fun. But it's got to be *good*. It can't be half-assed. They're paying money, man, and all that implies. They come to see you and you can't have an off night, even in Kansas City, because you are bringing a lot of people down. It's a lot easier to get a band together organically at the Matrix than it is at Madison Square Garden, where they are watching every note, every movement, "Is she gonna make it?" in their eyes.

Entropy's Terrible Whine

CONVERSATION breaks off abruptly as another round of drinks is ordered. These pauses allowed Janis to indulge in excruciating attacks of self-doubt. Her face would resume that expression of anguish which registered itself whenever she was monitoring herself. The little voices would speak up in intimidating rushes, as if the conversation had been listening to itself all along and had come up unexpectedly with a verdict.

Janis was a romantic and had little time for naturalism. Life that was unedited was also pointless; the mere succession of events was something to be overcome. It was an affront to her that all things and places and times should be equal before the indiscriminate rush of Time.

Like most of those whom she admired and emulated (Zelda, Mae West, Bessie Smith), Janis felt that style was everything. It was something she had refined through experience, although she knew it intuitively all along, and to her style meant form, everything that wasn't *simply* her, but those things she had grown to be; what she had made of what she was.

All the random, mindless hurrying of material and events was a humiliating and intolerable prospect and presented a very real terror to someone like Janis. She was afraid of losing control to the nameless forces of distintegration by letting herself be overwhelmed in the meaninglessness and absurdity of existence. She did not find mere moments in themselves illuminating, and she resented the possibility that these aimless, drifting conversations might, without reflection, dribble themselves, formless, into print, where they would bounce off the ear—as pointlessly as inchoate sounds reaching Jodrell Bank from space reflect the inane chatter of the universe.

Janis: I hope you're going to edit this stuff— I don't want to sound like a senile, self-pitying chick babbling on and on about her days of glory.

It doesn't sound like that at all.

It's like do you know what's wrong with most interviews? They're always too long, there's more stuff than you want to know.

People who dig you want to read every word.

I don't think so. It's like going to a movie, like *Woodstock,* I thought was a bad movie. It had a lot of good footage, but a movie is supposed to exercise taste and is supposed to be made by an artist, it has a flow like the way you write a story, it has a little peak at the beginning, a lull to grab you and hold you, and then another big climax, an ending. *Woodstock* doesn't have that, it just steam-rolls through, never goes up, never goes down, never knows when to stop, and neither do *Rolling Stone* interviews. *Cinéma vérité,* boring as hell. If you want to go to one I'll meet you at the corner bar after you're through, and I bet I'll be feeling better than you will. I know that things are shitty, but I'd rather laugh about it.

The Great Saturday Night Swindle

YOU *wrote the "Kozmic Blues," right?*

Yeah, I did write that one. I can't write a song unless I'm really traumatic, emotional, and I've gone through a few changes, I'm very down. No one's ever gonna love you any better and no one's gonna love you right. Maybe. Put you down. I like the song and I still believe in it to a degree, but I am still working on it. . . . I just realized, the other night, were you there? It's the first time it ever happened to me, I transcended the thing, I went into another stage, man . . . you know how on "Ball and Chain" I do that free-form ending, "Love is such a pain, love is such a pain . . ." that's what this new blues is about. "Move Over," about this man that I was in love with, he wouldn't be my old man but he wanted me to love him . . . men do that, they love to play that game, you know, taunt you with it . . . anyway at the end of that song it reminds me of an analogy of driving mules with a big long stick with a thing hanging with a carrot on it, you know, and they'd hold those things in front of the mule's nose, and those dumb mules keep going after it and never get it. That's what I

say at the end of the song I keep saying, "Like a carrot, baby, baby da-de-da-dum, like a carrot, baby." No one ever gets my imagery, that's the only trouble. No one ever listens to the words anyway. Fuck it. But I gotta hear it, I gotta believe it or I can't sing it. Anyway "Kozmic blues" was about some-one who loved me. As a matter of fact all my songs are. [*Laughs.*]

That's the blues, honey.

Waaall, man, when do I get the other side? People are always doing that to me, man. Oh man, it drives me up the fucking wall. People always come up to me, man, and say . . .

I think you ask for it, Janis.

I'm saying, Ooh man [*wailing*], I did every-thing I could for this cat, I really loved him . . . he was just like a one-day thing, a two-month thing, it was longer than that in actual fact . . . you know it's like any kind of rela-tionship where something hasn't worked out, you're sitting around—of course there's two sides to every issue—but you feel *hurt,* man [*starts wailing again*], oh man, why? Why'd he have to go and leave me like that, oh I'm so lonely oh-oh-oooh, and some guy'll come along and say, Well, it gives you more soul. Fuuuck you, man! [*Shouts*] I DON'T WANT ANYMORE! That's life.

"It's only a magazine . . . "

[*Sings*] "How much does it cost? It only costs a quarter. I've only got a nickel" But is it inherent? Do you really think it's in-herent? . . . because I *thiiink* . . . I'm not sure but I *think,* unless I'm fooling myself on one more level, I think that I think, at the very bottom . . . it's all a big joke [*laughs*] . . . on us.

The Kozmic Blues . . .

Yeah, the Kozmic Blues . . . first of all you've got to remember to spell it with a

"K." It's too down and lonely a trip to be taken seriously, it has to be a Crumb cartoon, like "White Man," it's like a joke on itself, I mean it'd have to be, but Kozmic Blues just means that no matter what you do, man, you get shot down anyway. Oh, I wanted to tell you what my new idea was, because I came up with it the other night while I was singing . . . I was talking about how love hurt you this way, love hurt you that way, now I just suddenly flashed . . . and I was writing a song about it, too . . . maybe it didn't hurt you because it wasn't supposed to last 25 years, maybe love can only be a day and still be love . . . like right now there's somebody being in love, then you ARE in love, you didn't get let down by love, you just have to spend the next few days and go to the movies! . . . I'm trying to write a song about, not get it while you can—it starts off that way—I mean get it while you can, and while you have it you *have* it. The Kozmic Blues doesn't exist, unless you have nothing. Kozmic Blues to me means . . . I remember when I was a kid they always told me, "Oh, you're unhappy because you're going through adolescence, as soon as you get to be a grownup everything's going to be cool." I really believed that, you know. Or, as soon as you grow up and meet the right man, or—if I could only get laid, if only I could get a little bread together, everything will be all right. And then, one day I finally realized it ain't all right and it ain't never gonna be all right, there's always something going wrong.

The world is a really sad place . . .

[*Angrily*] I know, but they never told me that when I was young! I always used the analogy of . . . I don't know if this is grossly insensitive of me, and it well may be, but like the black man's blues is based on the have-not—I got the blues because I don't have this, I got the blues because I don't have my baby, I got the blues because I don't have

the quarter for a bottle of wine, I got the blues because they won't let me in that bar. . . . Well, you know, I'm a middle-class white chick from a family that would love to send me to college and I didn't wanna. I had a job, I didn't dig it, I had a car, I didn't dig it, I had it real easy . . . and then one day I realized it in a flash sitting in a bar, that it wasn't an uphill incline that one day was going to be all right, it was your whole life. You'd never touch that fucking carrot, man, and that's what the Kozmic Blues are, cause you know you ain't never going to get it.

What keeps you going?

Work keeps you going. Being here is better than going to sleep, I guess.

Is it the thing that's missing that gives you the blues, or is it the nothing?

It's not the nothing, it's the want of something that gives you the blues. I mean if you don't mind sitting around with no clothes on, why you could be as happy as a loon. It's if you want to get dressed up, look spiffy, you got the blues; if you don't mind sitting in an apartment watching TV every night, you don't ever feel lonely, but if you want to be with someone and touch them, and talk to someone and hold them, and cook for them, then you are lonely. It's not what isn't, it's what you wish *was* that makes unhappiness. The hole, the vacuum . . . I think I think too much. That's why I drink.

It's a Capricorn failing.

What is? Drinking?

Yeah, that and thinking.

Drinkin and thinkin. I don't think it's Capricorn, I think it's people, and most of them think too much and they're all different sizes and shapes and they all figured it out. It all harkens back to when I was twenty, I figured it out. Got to get outta Texas, got to get outta

Texas, soon as I get outta Texas everything's gonna be okay. I ran away once, got fucked up, came back. Ran away again, made San Francisco, hung around bars. I couldn't get myself together, I didn't have many friends and I didn't like the ones I had, drinkin, sleepin in some little nickel-dime hotels in North Beach. I was sitting in the afternoon in a bar—I wasn't supposed to be there, I was twenty—I lied. I was sittin in there thinkin and suddenly it struck me like a fucking light bulb. That's all there was, man. I would probably be sitting in that bar, when I was eighty, saying *I can do* [*laughs*]; I can make it feel better, you know, whatever, so I wrote my father this big long letter because I am very close with my father—I'm not talking about now, because I haven't been home in a long time—a big long letter about how you guys always told me it was going to get better and I always thought it was an incline up that one day would level off. And you know, you mother fucker, it ain't leveling off, it's going to go straight up and when I'm eighty I'm going to die saying "I wonder if I did something wrong?" or some equally insecure, unaware trip, you know. I wrote my father this big long letter. There was only one other man in Port Arthur my father could talk to. My father was like a secret intellectual, a book reader, a talker, a thinker. He was very important to me, because he made me think. He's the reason I am like I am, I guess. He used to talk and talk to me and then he turned right around from that when I was fourteen—maybe he wanted a smart son or something like that—I can't figure that out. But he spent a long time talkin to me. The biggest thing in our house was when you learnt to write your name, you got to go and get a library card. He wouldn't get us a TV, he wouldn't allow a TV in the house. Anyway I wrote him this big long letter and a few months later I'd gone home, and he'd already showed this letter to the only other intellectual in town who was his best friend and they got together desperately and they just dug the fact that each other existed. This guy also dug me a lot and thought a lot of me, and my father showed him my letter, and when I came home this guy walked in—this was all new and confusing to me and startling . . . I felt God had played a joke on us and I was pissed off and everything, and this guy walked in with a sly smile on his face and he reached out his hand and said, "Well, Janis, I hear ya heard about the Great Saturday Night Swindle." I went whoooooh! I mean it's really true, huh? Here was a fifty-year-old man telling it like it is. I was proud of that. I talked about that all the time. . . . Out of the jumble of my life it's one of the few things I can remember clearly. I was always so stoned, and after a number of years everything seems to run together. Certainly things that matter you can remember. That's why I should stop drinking, because I think I'm missing a lot of good shows. But actually I want to be able to do it and not have drugs or booze or Coke be the reason I'm acting like that. I'm acting like that because I know how, straight. I never thought it would come to this. Something happened last year, and I became a grownup. I always swore I would never become a grownup no matter how old I got, but I think it happened. No sense worrying about it. Just rock on through.

What happened that made you decide that?

Just personal heavy changes. You have to do what comes naturally or it don't come out right, but people put me down for what I do too. That's my problem. I do that too much, just put it right out on the street, but you can't change because you become successful. Maybe it isn't wise though. Eric Clapton don't talk about his old lady, man. Nobody talks about their private pain. Nobody wants to know about it, man. I used to think, maybe they just had better press agents than me and kept it quiet. But then I realized that it's me. I talk too much. I haven't heard anyone else in the music business have their sheet . . . shit on the street . . . *sheet* on the street! Whew, tequila time [*laughs*]. Something my mother used to say: "Janis, think before you speak." And I used to say, "Why, why, man, because if I'm going to speak, why should I hold back?" Well, maybe there's something to be said for restraint. Maybe not in terms of truth but maybe in terms of common sense. See, maybe all those cats wouldn't be so scared of me, if I'd shut up, stop telling all I know, what I'm feeling—like that.

Janis, I think you should just keep going straight on. After awhile you realize you can't do anything else.

I realized it a long time ago, years before they even paid me to do it. Hey, I've met chicks who are doing me who can't even get a job as a stage hand because they won't change their style; take off all that jewelry, cover up their tattoos with makeup. They say, "Fuck you, man!" They ain't changing. I ain't changing. I was just lucky enough people wanted it, but who's to say what can always happen? But I don't care. I may not be drinking Rose Pueblo, I may be drinking port, but as long as I can buy my own bottle of wine, ain't nobody goin' to tell me what to do, man. Right?

Right!

Boy, I never said that before but it's true.

Sometimes, on the road, I watch you getting ready for a show . . .

Have you ever watched me hyping myself for a show?

Yeah, it's beautiful, like the deep knee bends.

I do more than that. I talk to myself, I loosen up my body . . . rapping on and on to myself, "Come on, honey, ooh, baby, blah-blah-blah-blah, *uhn!*" It's the same reason I run on when they announce me instead of just walking out there casually. I go whoooosh, so that by the time I get to the microphone my blood's goin bump-abump-abump-abump . . .
What were you saying, honey?

I was just going to say like everyday seems to be waiting for something to happen, something to get together . . .

You talkin about life or about music?

Both. It's like when you're on the road, everything becomes very immediate, condensed . . .

Right down to the truth. That's why I can't quit to become someone's old lady, cause I've had it so big . . . most women's lives are beautiful because they are dedicated to a man. I need him too, a lolling, loving, touching, beautiful man, but it can't touch, it can't even touch hitting the stage at full-tilt boogie. So I guess I'll stop at this. I'll take it. Can't do without it. Gimme that! [*Slaps, laughs.*]

What were you like before, I mean, before you discovered that?

Wide-eyed, bright-eyed, and bushy-tailed. Just a plain overweight chick. I wanted something more than bowling alleys and drive-ins. I'd've fucked anything, taken anything . . . I did. I'd take it, suck it, lick it, smoke it, shoot it, drop it, fall in love with it. . . . "Hey, man, what is it? I'll try it. How do you do it? Do you suck it? No? You swallow it? I'll swallow it." There's chicks like that right now, man. That little girl at the airport this morning, standing there in the rain, man. She reminded me of me when I was that age. Seven or eight years of doing that shit, man. It's strange, you know that? What strange, weird events took me to this

place. Chances, strokes of bad luck. Bad fortune a year later would turn into good fortune. Who would know what it was about? The musical climate, events, falling out in that way, every fucking conceivable thing brought it all together to make this strange person, this chick who was good at this one thing, man, just this one fucking thing. I lost a lot along the way. I may never get it back. But I know I ain't quittin. It's just strange to think the kind of person I ended up, you know? Everybody looks back when they're a few years older and says, "God, how did this happen? How did I turn into this person, man?"

Like when you see an old photo of yourself . . .

Yeah, sometimes I look at my face and I think it looks pretty run down, but considering all I been through, I don't look bad at all.

I think you look very together, Janis.

Really, man? You silver-tongued devil, you. [*Laughs.*]

You look healthy.

When I was a junkie I didn't look too good. You remember what I looked like in England last year? I looked this young, but I looked gray, I looked defeated. I kept it together on stage, but it didn't come anywhere near being as good as the first shows in Kansas City this year, because that was real. It was a boogie and they knew it. That's why I've been looking so good lately. I haven't felt so good since the time I made it with Big Brother. The last year, year and a half, I've been going through a lot of personal changes. I was a junkie, for one thing, but that wasn't it. That wasn't the cause of it, that was the result. I was afraid I was fooling them, and they'd find out. I think I decided just recently with my music, "Don't play it, don't lie it, if you're going to do it, be it! Try it! You're not dumb, try, Janis!" You know, these last couple of months I finally accepted I could do it.

"Blues Is an Aching Old Heart Disease"

BY THIS TIME Bob Neuwirth has arrived and Janis begins gathering up her feathers to leave. Conversations drift aimlessly about, each submerged in their own liquid zones. A bearded man in his late 30's approaches the table unsteadily as if he had just wandered in from North Beach with a hurriedly packed suitcase of unsatisfied longings. I realize with some alarm that we are in the vague world of repetitions that is the condition of most bars, conversations which eddy around their own extinction, full of blurs and clumps that begrudgingly extend their private reality to the outside. Janis's travels were full of such enigmatic encounters. Mercurial, tutelary figures, like the good shepherd or ferryman that populate the adventures of heroes of folk tales, would approach her with amulets and advice, familiars swarming with half-forgotten roles would awake, suddenly released by the semiconscious flux of the evening, and attach themselves to Janis with the fixity of images in a dream where reunions take place between half-realized secrets about the things and people of this world. Even the secularization of time has not been able to sweep away this litter of epiphanies that accumulates under the pressure of the

day and seeps back at night to break up the matrices of reality. The bearded man, "North Beach," slumps down at the table bringing his own conversation with him. His labored syllables and exploding consonants give his words the cadence of nursery rhymes.

NORTH BEACH: Ya know I ne-ver heard Billie in person . . .

JANIS: I never did either, man, course I was a girl . . .

NORTH BEACH: I had a chance to see her—she made several appearances where I was living—then I heard she died, and then I realized I blew it.

JANIS: I can dig it.

NORTH BEACH: She's now part of my music; of course you're part of my music now, too.

JANIS: Shucks.

NORTH BEACH: I didn't know such a young girl could do it! [*Laughs*] Little kid like you.

JANIS: Young upstart like me.

NORTH BEACH: Young upstart like *you*.

JANIS: [*Seriously*] Well, we do the best we can . . . If you think I'm good now, wait ten years, boy, I'll blow your fuckin mind. Whoooo! [*Stamps her feet and shrieks.*] If I ain't ten years better than this ten years from now, you know, I'm gonna start selling dope again, turning a few tricks on the side, to keep my shit together.

NORTH BEACH: You took a coupla litta tips from Bessie and Billie . . .

JANIS: Musically?

NORTH BEACH: Besides musically . . . you already have the tips from them. . . .

JANIS: What d'ya mean?

NORTH BEACH: Don't fall too hard.

JANIS: I-don't-think-I-got-that-one.

NORTH BEACH: *Don't*-kill-yourself.

JANIS: Maybe that's why you like them so much . . . I don't think that's why you like them so much, but I think it may contribute to the romantic mystique . . . it's intriguing . . .

NORTH BEACH: Are you as good as they are?

JANIS: I know one thing . . .

NORTH BEACH: I liked Billie long before she died. Bessie died about the year I was born, so I couldn't say whether I liked her or not before she died . . .

JANIS: I can tell you one thing I know just from getting interviewed so many times, man [*to me*] this has nothing to do with you, honey, is that people, whether they know it or not, they like their blues singers miserable.

NORTH BEACH: They like their blues singers miserable and drunk.

JANIS: They like their blues singers to die afterwards.

NORTH BEACH: Dying and dead.

JANIS: Man, I've had interviewers come up to me . . .

NORTH BEACH: There's no reason for it, there's no reason for it . . .

JANIS: Well, I ain't doin' nothin', I ain't doin' shit for them, man—I've had interviewers come up with a microphone to me and say, "Tell me, Janis, you think you'll die a young and unhappy death?" [*Cackles.*] Well, I say, "I hope not, man!"

NORTH BEACH: You know, you should be on WBAI—have a round-table kind of thing where nobody is out to ask you are you thinking of dying young or why do you drink so much.

JANIS: Sure havin' a good time, man.

NORTH BEACH: You sure do drink a helluva lot, don't you?

JANIS: What?

NORTH BEACH: You do drink a lot.

JANIS: I do. I do the best I can.

NORTH BEACH: You ought to watch it in the next couple years.

JANIS: Oh, man!

NORTH BEACH: The pace. Slow down, you finally realize you're doing yourself in.

JANIS: I figured that out a long time ago. I also figured this: I gotta go on doin it the way I see it. Hey, man, I ain't got no choice but to take it like I see it. I'm a fucking human being, man, can you understand that? I'm here to have a party, man, as best as I can while I'm on this earth. I think it's your duty to. When I'm ready to retire I'll tell you about it. If I start worrying about everything I'm doing, you know, like—like this'll give you cholesterol or cirrhosis or some other dumb, unaware trip, I'd just as soon quit now. If that's what I gotta do to stick around another forty years, you can have it. Hey, listen, man, I plan on being around a long time, but that's the only fuckin thing I'm planning on. Let it happen, man! I'm gettin it now, today, I don't even know where I'm gonna be twenty years from now, so I'm just gonna keep on rockin, cause if I start saving up bits and pieces of me like that, man, there ain't gonna be nothing left for Janis.

ENTRAIN'D SEAS

Let the reader consider what he would give . . . to stay
the cloud in its fading, the leaf in its trembling, and the
shadows in their changing; to bid the fitful foam be fixed
upon the river, and the ripples be everlasting upon the
lake; and then to bear away with him no darkness or
feeble sun-stain, but a counterfeit which should seem no
counterfeit—the true and perfect image of life indeed.
Or rather, let him consider that it would be in effect
nothing less than the capacity of transporting himself at
any moment into any scene—a gift as great as can be
possessed by a disembodied spirit; and suppose, also, this
necromancy embracing not only the present but the past,
and enabling us seemingly to enter into the bodily presence of men long since gathered to the dust; to behold
them in act as they lived . . . to see them in the gesture
and expression of an instant, and stayed on the eve of
some great deed, in the immortality of burning purpose.
—JOHN RUSKIN, *Frondes Agrestes*

ENTRAIN'D SEAS

Is It Rolling, Bob?

Oooey, hooey . . . I'm just dreamin dreams,
Oooey, hooey . . . I'm just dreamin dreams,
The whole roun world is mine,
Things are not like they seem . . .
—Little Brother Montgomery, "Lake Front Blues"

JUST AS GRAVITY and the pressure of light give form to stars and galaxies, so Time seems to shape the things and events that we have known in little clusters that move around a still center. This is most true of daydreams that circle lazily but with the precision of spirals around certain memories that we locate in specific places only out of convenience. At a great distance, like looking down an infinite thread of track, even these spaces in which the original memories formed themselves begin to resemble one another, and so, the spaces in which we have daydreamed re-create themselves in a new daydream.

In the Rally Room of the York Hotel in Calgary, Alberta, a hundred musicians and friends are trying to re-create the daydream of a recent five-day journey (between June 29th and July 3rd, 1970, to locate it precisely in time, and in space between Toronto and Calgary. Method of conveyance: train). Ian and Sylvia, the Good Brothers, Bob Weir, David Torbet and Marmaduke of the New Riders of the Purple Sage are singing country songs, but tonight the musicians are remote, huddled in corners. It's an attempted evocation, as if we were all back again in one of the lounges of the train where people sat down together and joined in the music. Everyone is trying to re-create the train's spaces in this institutional square-shaped reception hall, like the anniversary party in that Czech film. The illusion comes and goes as groups of people stand around tables piled with sandwiches.

"Is this the bar car?" Janis asks, entering the room like an explosion, and everyone catches himself momentarily in an automatic reflex to the rocking of an imaginary train. Janis was the presiding spirit of this journey, the Bacchanalian Little Red Riding Hood with her bag full of tequila and lemons, lurching from car to car like some tropical bird with streaming feathers, defying the sun to interrupt our revels with another day.

Janis's conversation is full of suggestion. She is familiar with the illusion of the flux of time and ballsy enough to defy it by implication. For her there is only one party, and wherever it occurs, that's the only thing that ever happened. The gears of time grind to a halt as Janis uncorks another bottle of tequila with its symbolic eagle ("He who understands has wings"). She knew that the greatest property of alcohol is its ability to abolish time, and with it its tattletale, memory. When you're afloat in its heady bath, memory seems to be no more than the regret of certain moments. The morning after the great *Million Dollar Bash* ("I got the Dead drunk," Janis cackles triumphantly) that took place on the last night on the train, Jerry Garcia stumbled out into the daylight, brilliant blue as a constable's uniform, groaning in a parody of the amnesiac drunk, "I promise never to drink again, your Honor. How's my head? I need a lobotomy."

There's only our suitcases to remind us that we are at the terminus rather than on the train in this journey without tickets, our pockets still full of wishes. Janis is the tutelary spirit of the evening as on the train, refusing to accept the conditions of adult life (which always involve some submission to the drab terrors of Time) by passing from childhood to childhood, using an occasional substitute mother to moor herself when times got bad. Janis's spell, her great command of temporary disequilibrium, was always a childhood one, an ability to hoodwink the spirits of the moment and recover the lost Kingdom of Pleasure not only for herself but for anyone who would set sail with her for an evening in her tippled glassy boat. The feathers, the bells, the slingback shoes often looked suspiciously *mature* on Janis, like a child's put-on. Even the way she shuffled about in her pointy heels gave her whole out-fit the effect of dressing up. And so it was on this night that we all fell back for a few moments into the cradling rhythm of the train under the influence of spirits and songs. "We're only a handful of miles from Calgary now," says Sam Cutler, sliding aboard this imaginary locomotive. "It's all down to shortage of women, that's what it is," he adds tapping an unattached mood.

Janis hands him a bottle of tequila and a wedge of lemon. "Ugh! Foul stuff," he says as he completes the ritual. "But it has magic properties," Jerry Garcia tells him, with the Dead's personal understanding of alchemy. "It's made from cactus. It's got to have a little bit of that *thing* in it, Sam. You know, desert food."

"This is the only way to travel, stoned," Janis says, cackling at her own joke. But even Janis cannot bring back the presence of the train completely, and the party drifts into dejected little bunches. Rounds of songs start up again, and Janis, like a defiant helmsman, balances herself on a slope of the room as we guide ourselves through the treacherous crags and reefs of the ominous present. On the choruses of songs we pull against the gigantic tide with voices like overlapping oars, ghostly rowers gliding gently back in time.

Janis interrupts her juggling of moments. A sudden flush of apprehension takes hold of her. Someone is not helping to row the clunking memory ship through the heavy seas of the evening. "I want to see what these guys are talking about," she says, challenging Jonathan Cott and me across the crowded room. "Hey, man, what does *Rolling Stone* talk about to itself?" she asks, conveniently rolling us up into a collective proper noun. As it happens we'd been talking about Sweet Marie, which in Canada is a candy bar.

"Well, Janis, we were just thinking maybe Dylan wrote that song, you know, 'Where are you tonight, Sweet Marie?'—well, that maybe he wrote it about a candy bar," I say, holding the wrapper gingerly. "Is that what you guys talk about, really? Is that all, man?" she says in disgust and slightly disappointed that her own paranoia has not been justified. "At least you could've been talking about *me,* you fuckers. . . ."

And, as if recoiling from the inevitable, the hopelessness of *actually* reversing the order of things, Janis wails into Merle Haggard's mournful "The Bottle Let Me Down." In the corner, Rick Danko is singing some Miracles songs with Buddy Guy's bass player, and as the notes spill into the half-empty room lined with chairs, as at high school dance, the participants in this extraordinary adventure take themselves off, like children wistfully looking back, aware that its suspended moments are gone forever.

Each night I leave the bar when it's over,
Not feeling any pain at closing time,
But tonight your memory found me much too sober
Couldn't drink enough to keep you off my mind.

I've always had a bottle I could turn to,
And lately I've been turning every day,
But the wine don't take effect the way it used to,
Now I'm hurtin' in an old familiar way.

Tonight the bottle let me down
And let your memory come around.
The one true friend I thought I'd found
Tonight the bottle let me down
Tonight the bottle let me down.
  —Merle Haggard, "The Bottle Let Me Down"

Trains of Thought

IF TIME IS the negative element in the sensual world, then the Festival Express (whose passengers consisted of Janis and the Full Tilt Boogie, the Grateful Dead, Delaney and Bonnie and friends, Buddy Guy's band, Ian and Sylvia and the Great Speckled Bird, Eric Andersen, Tom Rush, James and the Good Brothers, the New Riders of the Purple Sage, Robert Charlebois, Mashmakhan, and Rick Danko of the Band) seemed, like Monterey, to unfold in some sense in the infinite time in which childhood exists. Janis with her usual perceptiveness had seen it from the beginning. "The train is Mother," she said. "It's the best time I've had since I left Port Arthur." It wasn't just a special time for all of us, it was the reestablishment of the lost condition of childhood.

Man is the woman revealed as the child
Concealed in a handful of play

Bob Carpenter sang, as a fitting epitaph for the trip. Bob was a guitarist who mysteriously showed up at the York Hotel where the farewell party was taking place.

The train trip, in fact, allowed the performers to enter the kind of traveling energy people used to discover in themselves as they entered their music. Now, for the musicians, the train embodied that state in which Bachelard once wrote, "The warm substance of intimacy resumes its form, the same form that it had when it enclosed original warmth."

The passengers were reluctant to get off the train when it came to its final destination, as if they were saying goodbye to something of themselves. For the time being, anyway, everything was flattened into the present. This you could deduce from the fact that the days seemed almost indistinguishable from one another, just one long day, except for the shifting backdrops of pine and water outside the windows.

Thoughts about the journey recall the same remote and perfect climate of childhood, as I have said, and I can still see the train in its entire length in perfect clarity as if it were an exact replica of itself. At any moment I can peer into its windows like the little glassine windows of clockwork trains and examine its perfectly embalmed interiors, tiny lamps glued slightly askew on waxy tables with places set permanently with diminutive knives and spoons.

Right now I can see through the window of the bar car. Janis and Rick Danko are listening to Eric Andersen singing a weightless song that sounds as if it were translated from another dimension, while outside the window the plains of Saskatchewan spread out forever like a two-million-hole golf course.

I was dreaming now I look so pale
Dying was easy, hear the darkness wail
I was sailing without a sail.

We looked so lovely sometimes
Like children out in the dawn of time
I just fell back into my mind.
                    —Eric Andersen, "A Dream to Rimbaud,"
                                    United Artists Music

Outside the land is a platform of vegetable hallucinations. Flatland trees stunted by prevailing winds. "That barn just yawned," someone says as we pass by a perfect red-and-white prairie barn. Its white loft window stares back at us in surprise like an illustration from a children's book.

"You can get drunk just looking out the window," Eric says about the displaced sense of time and space that has infected everyone on this journey. Like holidays, dreams, memories, utopias, songs, there has been little to remind us of our environments, of specific places, of time in its mordant aspect.

The Blushful Hippocrene

WORDS, someone once said, are a halfway house to lost things, and in this daydream Jonathan conducts his interview with the train as it suns itself, like the articulated shell of some prehistoric animal by the gloomy shores of a Canadian lake.

COTT: How are you enjoying this trip?
TRAIN: Beautiful, man. The music inside me makes me feel really good, a strange feeling, though, you know, R 'n' B in the intestines, country music in the chest. It keeps away that empty feeling I sometimes get on the regular trip.
COTT: Have you been keeping track of Janis? Pardon the pun.
TRAIN: The Whale had Jonah and I've got

Janis. A grand lady. As Eric Andersen said, I'd give her my last sip. She knows how to survive. Gets up in the morning and gets moving. Like me, I can relate to that. My steam-engine brothers didn't make it. But I just keep moving. Janis gets me feeling heady, like that old poem:

O for a beaker full of the warm South,
  Full of the true, the blushful Hippocrene,
    With beaded bubbles winking at the brim,
      And purple-stained mouth;
That I might drink, and leave the world unseen,
And with thee fade away into the forest dim.

Yeh, that's Janis now, winking at the brim.
COTT: We'd like to find out about your origins, your influences.
TRAIN: Well, it was all Asa Whitney's dream. I can't go back that far, like there's this haze and chimeras, something real ahead, and that was all Asa's dream. You know that it's just 101 years since that golden spike was driven into the rail at Promontory, Utah, where the Central and Union Pacific came together. But I always feel that moving through Canada now is what it must have been like going across the States then. Lots of people inside me today opened their windows, looked through me, and decided to move up here. Just look at the mauve-and-mother-of-pearl sunset up ahead. Just dreams to remember.

The Angel's Trumpet Speaks and Janis Sleeps

THE WHEELS of memory spin us back, and without hesitation the train obliges us by pulling on a pair of trousers made up especially for the afternoon as it strides jauntily off among a cloud of names, little towns, some scarcely more than a huddle of shacks, that we pass through on the way evoking the mystery of unknowable places. The nostalgic transplants from the suburbs of London: Islington, Tottenham, Bayswater, Bethnal; French trapper posts: Foleyet, Lainaune, Girouxville, La Broquerie; Iroquois names: Kawa, Kowkash, Unaka, Minnipuka, Paqwa, Penequani; and crazy wilderness names that trail into each other like a serial poem: Ophir, Snakesbreath, Decimal, Malachi, Forget.

Its moments flash past deliciously close (but sealed in that dangerous zone of time where collapsed memories are stored) like the windows of an express speeding by at night, each lighted window a fraction of that sequence automatically stored in the flush of a moment waiting to be retrieved as a lucky hand of cards.

Janis is reading in her compartment, another chapter of her transmigrations. "Look homeward, Angel" it whispers with the poisonous lips of the datura (Angel's Trumpet) that Zelda liked to paint in her madness, scorning the more obvious roses and violets in the garden in Montgomery. And there will be those who wonder, too, like the old woman on the portico, "Where was she that she could not come back: where did she go? Where?" And I, too, cannot see her in all the squandering of hours and days. Among all the wastes of time, surely there is a blind spot that would give access to a moment, like the reversal of a grammatical construction where we could visit ourselves and those that were with us.

In another car a session shifts to an up-tempo blues with Bonnie and Buddy Guy trading verses: "Knockin' on my door, don't want me around no more . . ." "Forget it and let this trouble pass . . ." Delaney's horns join in, and A. C. Reed (Jimmy Reed's brother) from Buddy's band pumps a fat

Detroitish sound from his sax. The music slows down to a slow boogie in late afternoon as we pull into a small town.

Capreol: A telephone-wire cat's cradle above the tracks, tract houses shingled in creosote imitation brick skulking around the station. As we glide between the soot-black CNR oil tanks, the music grinds to a lugubrious funeral step, like a New Orleans street band.

Our first stop since leaving Toronto. Sam Cutler scrambles down the gravel bank to the dirt track that is the main road in Capreol, looking to score. He comes across an ice cart being wheeled to the train, tests the ice, which is used for cooling the compartments, and heads for town.

Downtown Capreol is two opened stores: a food store and the Oriental Emporium Variety Shop, run by a Chinese family that sells mountain dew.

Sam happily goes off with an eight-dollar shimmering kimono of many colors and ten packages of Smarties candies. By the side of the train station and down a sand dune is a lake suited for beavers and black flies, intersected by a row of joining pieces of lumber. Delaney and Bonnie's sax and horn men play a lonesome Dixieland duet at the water's edge, while musicians skipper stones. Six teen-age girls are standing by the train looking for Janis, who's asleep.

A Kiss for the Boys from Manitoba

THE FARTHER west you travel in the prairies, the more squashed down and nubbed the trees seem in this unrelieved flatness, stunted by the prevailing winds. Grass grows up between the tracks.

Arbitrarily we stop the train at Winnipeg,

and, obedient to the willfulness of memory, the train exhales a cloud of steam and grinds to a halt.

The Winnipeg Depot is a flat industrial area about four miles from the center of town. Brick and cement buildings—facades of a displaced industrial revolution—stood in an open space overgrown with weeds, suggesting the disconcerting familiarity of dreams where the geometric syntax is dislocated: a monstrous 19th-century pump behind a wall of green glass, a cement signal box, sheds and platforms. "Welcome to Omaha!" says Sam Cutler.

Jerry Garcia walks down the tracks singing a country blues he is just completing. The film crew closes in, pleased to be shooting in daylight for a change, and captures a few solarized moments.

"Believe it or not, I helped lay this section of track, hammered in these spikes right here," says Frank Duckworth, publicist for the Festival Express, making the anonymous stretch of track as vivid as a piece of the true cross. "People forget what goes into a track. They laid this section during the Depression, 75 cents a day for breaking your back in humid 95-degree weather."

Duckworth speaks almost laconically, like an urbane Bill Cody, but the words bring up a host of sweating images all reduced to this unassuming thread of metal that abstracts 4,000 miles from Nova Scotia to the Pacific. He picks a squat green plant from behind the track. "Know what this is? Lambs quarters. You soon get to know your weeds when you're starving like we were back in the days of '29, '30. Makes a delicious salad and it grows just about anywhere. They used to feed us a staple diet of prunes—CNR strawberries, we used to call them."

The idea of the Festival Express, a train trip across Canada, is Duckworth's. He talks of the railroads with deep affection.

"Trains are almost all freight today, and it's a pity, because they were a very elegant, leisurely form of transportation. In a plane you have no sensation of traveling at all, it's like being pushed through a tube, a very sterile, inhuman experience. Imagine the opulence and tastefulness of traveling in those days. Did you ever see the carriage Queen Victoria traveled in when she made her state visit to Canada? Tassels and velvet, padded and tuffetted like a case for the Czar's Easter eggs."

Janis steps down from the train, a blur of colors, as her red and blue bows gently brush against her face in the light wind. "Morning, boys," she says, crossing the tracks to the buses that had come to take us into town.

A local hippie warns us that the mood in Winnipeg isn't too friendly. "They're burying the chief of police today," he says. "Some guy shot him and two other fuzz down in this alley, and the cat they're questioning supposedly is claiming he was high on acid." Today was also Canada's centenary, and Pierre Trudeau, the Prime Minister, was in Winnipeg to give a speech.

Janis, Marmaduke, and Eric Andersen set off for town and Tiny Tim's bar. Longhairs are shifting around the town square waiting for Trudeau to arrive, and Janis and Eric offer everyone a moment's unexpected entertainment by wading through the fountain.

The stadium where the Festival is to perform is right next to a midway, where barkers entice the simple plains people into their grotesque booths. "See the horror of the electric chair"; "the incredible half elephant, half pig"; "the body of a 2,000-year-old man preserved in ice"; "vicious rats devouring a live python." Next to this exotic cosmos of freaks, a festival seems tame.

The crowd barely fills the front of the stadium, but it is an enthusiastic one. Charlebois gets a good reception, although he is singing mainly in French. There is a large French community here, in fact, and at mid-

night there is a Cajun music festival held on the banks of the Bow River.

To add to the problems at Winnipeg a strong wind picks up during the afternoon, blowing spirals of dust into everyone's faces. A sudden gust blows the Good Brothers' drum kit right off the stage. It is like those sudden Midwestern dust storms blowing up into tornadoes, and as the concert ends, with paper cups swirling off the ground in little pools of air, it seems that the currents may sweep us all away into another Oz.

Janis closes the show, and her set is remarkable under the circumstances. In the middle of "Maybe" a burly cowboy jumps onto the stage and asks for a "kiss for the boys from Manitoba," as in some scene from an old Dietrich movie. Janis obliges, and as he's leaving the stage, the delirious embodiment of Manitoba thanks the stage hands for letting him through. "Why are you thanking them, honey?" Janis asks in her plaintive voice. "They didn't do nothing for you!"

Toward the Great Divide

The train trip wasn't a dream, it was a stone boss reality. I'm still on the train. I just turn on the switch, and the fan's on, and the train's still moving.
—Pigpen

ALTHOUGH there is a certain perverse pleasure involved in interrupting its progress at various points (one irresistible moment when the mayor of Calgary, like the Pied Piper announces to the Festival promoter, Ken Walker, "Let the children of Calgary pass through the gates free," and

Walker shouts back at the mayor, "I don't care if you're king, I'm from Toronto!"), there is a special pleasure in beginning at the beginning, letting the train puff laboriously out of the Toronto marshaling yard in that almost imperceptible moment with its as yet unformulated contents of people and events.

The train is waiting for us at the Toronto Coach yard: a slick modern diesel, twelve coaches long with "Festival Express" painted in orange and black ten-foot letters on the baggage car. "She's a born speedster, more like a bullet than a kettle," an old brakeman confides to us as we creep aboard furtively as hoboes riding the freight, at the dimly lit station in the early hours of Monday morning. Before setting off we are asked to sign a waiver which says in part that we will "keep the Festival Express from any harm or danger that may present itself," and for an instant we flash on ambushes by hostile bands of Sioux and Blackfeet or hordes of buffalo swarming the tracks like a sea of fur.

And to look at the company of cowboys boarding the train—the Grateful Dead in their rodeo boots, embossed "Nudie" belts, sheath knives, and hoedown shirts from Miller's Western Store in Denver, James and the Good Brothers in Wrangler suits, and the Riders of the Purple Sage decked with the unmistakable ciphers of the genuine cowhand—it is possible to imagine that we're all setting off on some perilous journey toward the Great Divide.

Once inside the sleeping cars, given dreamlike names—Valparaiso, Beausejour, Etoile—the illusion of the Great Iron Horse pushing westward into unchartered land is destroyed by the stainless-steel-baked enamel surfaces of the train's interior. Early arrivals are checking out the tiny sleeping compartments: "Man, I've been in jail cells larger than this," a Marin County voice shouts.

The little boxlike rooms with neat blue curtains stretch down the length of the sleeping cars like space-age opium dens, or a hygienic modern bordello. Each cubicle is about 3 by 6 feet and a technological miracle. A galaxy of instruments and conveniences are insanely compressed into this tiny column of space: a large blue couch, a bed, a toilet, washbasin, jump seat, ice-water dispenser with paper cups, a drainless washbasin that folds away used water magically into some receptive crevice (stainless steel sleight of hand), a clothes closet, an air conditioner, a fan, a cupboard and clusters of metallic outgrowths: ashtrays, hooks, handles, clips and catches.

All this compression is relieved by a giant window that spans the width of the compartment like an 8mm movie screen registering the trees, lakes and rivers outside at 24 frames per second. In essence, the cubicles are both sleeping tubes and meditation chambers where the musicians spend quiet hours, between the orgies of music in the lounges, writing songs, practicing, rapping, getting stoned. The compact space encourages daydreaming, but its closeness forces you out into the lounges and bar cars to participate in what's going on in the world of the train.

The ingenuity of the room's design is also the source of endless Chaplinesque situations: bodies bobbing in and out of the compartments, bumping, tripping, spilling into the aisles in various states of mind and undress. Marx Brothers slapstick exits and entrances are reenacted in the early morning hours as stoned, drunk, wiped-out occupants attempt to deal with the machine in comic desperation.

To get into bed means stepping out of the room, because pulling the bed out means filling the whole space in the compartment. But once you're in bed, wanting to use the washbasin or the john involves getting out into the corridor again, closing the bed, using the basin, re-closing it, going out into the hall a second time, and finally pulling down the bed. As the Drunken Train lurches its way through the sparsely inhabited continent, this mechanical ritual reaches the level of high farce. Janis emerges early one afternoon about the third day out triumphantly announcing she has discovered her washbasin while looking for a place to hang her clothes.

On the first night aboard the passengers make their acquaintance with each other in the dining car, where a buffet of triangular sandwiches has been laid on. The atmosphere is cautious, almost morosely quiet. Delaney and Bonnie play poker for octagonal Canadian nickels, and Steve Knight, Mountain's organist, bemoans the fact that he didn't bring his Monopoly set. "Thirty-six hours of this is really going to flip us out," someone says. The awkward encounters have the overtones of the first day of summer camp, where everyone hangs around waiting for something to happen. A subtle panic creeps up on everyone: five days stuck on a train with nowhere to go and nothing to do but look at 130 other freaks. Better to crash at Holiday Inn.

A few people start to drift into the forward lounge. Leslie West and Felix Pappalardi pull out guitars. West, toying with his tiny ancient Les Paul Gibson as if it were a stalk of grass, lazily picks out Delta bottleneck blues, and Mountain's drummer, Corky Laing, sings along: "Let it rain, let it pour/ And let it rain some more/ Got those deep river blues." Jerry Garcia, Delaney, and Kenny Gradney, Delaney's bass player, join in, and as the swarm of guitars picks up to a resonating hum, it becomes obvious what we will be doing for the next week.

From early Monday morning until we finally get off the train in Calgary five days later, the music stops only once—when everyone gets off at Winnipeg for the Festival. Buddy Guy's drummer, Roosevelt, immacu-

late in his flashy snakeskin suit, plays for two days straight, and it's a common thing to fall out, get up, have breakfast, and get back to the lounge to find the same "set" rocking on. The Festival Express is the reenactment of a piece of blues mythology; the box-car studio, where drifters like Bumble Bee Slim and Tampa Red, with harmonica and dobros, hopped the Illinois Central from New Orleans or the M & O from Mobile up to Memphis, St. Louis and Chicago, on trains with names like the Panama Limited, the Flying Crow, Midnight Special, Green Diamonds, Rock Island Line now resonant with blues connotations, incorporating the clicking steel rhythms of the train and the shrill "quills" of the fireman's whistle into lazy Delta harmonies:

Flying Crow leaves Port Arthur,
calls at Shreveport to change her crew,
She will take water at Texarkana,
yes, boys, and keep on through.

That Flying Crow whistle sounds so lonesome and sad,
Lord, it broke my heart, and took the last woman I had.
                —Washboard Sam, "Flying Crow Blues"

Seducer, Ark, destroyer, and mother (Mickey Mouse was born on a train), a verb in a world of towns, the train called others, too, just as it whistled Janis out of Texas. Bette Davis in *Beyond the Forest* heard its hooded voice beckoning: "Come Rosa, come away, Rosa, before it's too late," the train seemed to say. "Chic-a-go, Chic-a-go."

"The train is like the guitar, man," said Willie Dixon. You know, when you look down those tracks from the caboose? You see the ties closing up like the frets on the guitar. The further you get from the Delta, the higher up you're playing on the neck. In Chicago, baby, we're really wailing!"

As blue phosphorous lights settle on the marshaling yard, the Riders of the Purple Sage (Marmaduke, Dave Nelson and Dave

Torbert, who form part of the Dead's 20-member family on the train) unpack their Gibsons, and blues give way to country: Hank Williams, Merle Haggard, Kris Kristofferson.

Eventually people drift off and fall out. We wake up the next morning in the forests of northern Ontario: an infinity of lakes and rivers cut into a wilderness of birch trees. On both sides, fields of daisies, trillium and buttercups curve up from the verge of the tracks. Giant copper-red boulders seem to squeeze the train as it passes through them, and sheets of rock, flat as mirrors, refract the harsh northern light that edges every stone and leaf and tree. Swirls and eddies of water wash around white tree trunks, half submerged, and islands that slope down to find white gravel. There are so many lakes, it seems one map cannot contain them, and stands of birch and elm so immense, in this land inhabited only by water, trees, animals and clouds, that images practically assault the eye.

In the lounge, where a session composed of musicians who had been playing all night (Janis clutching her bottle like a baby) and some who have just got up, is still in full swing, the images within and without multiply, and looking down the length of the car, the windows on both sides give the illusion of looking into a giant stereopticon that by some trick of light and space seems to suspend the musicians in an unreal landscape.

Every Fool Has His Rainbow

JOSTLING DOWN the corridors to the bar car, or the lounge, as the train lazily noses its way through the pine barrens of Saskatchewan,

sounds reach out to grab you from every compartment you pass. You might find Clark practicing drum riffs, horn players blowing the old familiar runs—Charlie Parker, Hendricks and Ross—Buddy Guy and a Cajun fiddler laughing and playing, the Good Brothers singing together in that old hillbilly way, Jerry Garcia and John Cooke (Janis's road manager and no mean country singer) harmonizing and exchanging songs, Janis, like a hedonistic Queen Victoria sipping gin, cackling away with some friends in her compartment, while in the next compartment, behind closed curtains, Flatt and Scruggs are playing on someone's cassette recorder, and everything is blending together, the tracks clicking underneath and almost above the music—and the train.

In the bar car, hardly as wide as most people's hallways, little groups of people swirl on egg-cup chairs, letting the evening drift over them. "Bring me another screwdriver, honey," Janis calls out, holding court, like Mother Goose, to a little gathering.

"I hope there aren't gonna be any operas on this train," says the bartender, looking up from his book, *The Rainbow Trail.* "The guy who was on from Toronto said there was a lot of noise."

"Nothing to worry about," Janis says. "The Who aren't on this trip." He doesn't understand, but Janis howls with a laugh as wide as Texas, and he falls into it.

"Whoooh! There's so much *talent* on this train," Janis says, laughing at her own double entendre. "I *knew* it was going to be a party, man. I didn't take this gig for nothing else but that. I said, 'It sounds like a party, and I wanna be there. It's gonna be Rockin Pneumonia and Boogie Woogie Flu . . . wow!' "

"Holy cow, watcha doin chile, / Holy smoke, it ain't no joke . . ." Rick and Janis were wailing Lee Dorsey, Rick harmonizing with his Dodge City whine. After a few more old favorites like "I Kept the Wine and Threw Away the Rose," "Silver Threads and Golden Needles," and "Honeysuckle Rose," Eric sang a song that *he* wrote on the train— a subtle, quiet song that Janis's voice understood intuitively: "Do you remember the night I cried for you, do you remember the night I cried for you . . . ?"

"Are we in Calgary yet?" Janis asked as we hit the outskirts of Saskatoon.

"Whoopee," John Cooke yodeled in his finest Western manner. "The next town we git to, we're going to divest it of its young womanhood!"

Everybody piled off the train and descended on the railroad souvenir shop, hungry for cultural trash: lurid magazines, sleazy paperbacks, candy-kitsch pastel emblems depicting beavers and leaping salmon painted on felt, postcards with Mounties, Indian chiefs, and moose (legend on the back reads, "Mounted, this fine head makes an excellent wall hanging for club, office, or recreation room"). The owners couldn't believe it. A horde of freaks snatching up every piece of junk in the store! But to the denizens of L.A. and Marin County, Saskatoon is as exotic as Outer Mongolia.

Meanwhile, John Cooke and Festival Express coordinator Dave Williams made a run on the town liquor store. They slammed down $400 on the counter: "Tell us when it's used up," they said, like a couple of prospectors come to drink up their claim.

The "claim" was hoisted on board, and the "People's Bar" was set up. It now included a giant totemic gallon-sized bottle of Canadian Club which seemed like the symbol of All Drink, and by the time the Million Dollar Bash was over, would "prove the strongest man at last."

The party gradually drifts into the lounges. Janis spots a long-haired kid standing alone on the platform. "Get on, man," she shouts, miming through the window, but he just smiles and waves as the train pulls out of the station.

As we left the town behind, the band picked up, rhythm got a little faster. The wheels were turning over like a steel metronome under us, clicking off time as relentlessly as a Rhythm King, the meter of our thoughts, an invisible envelope of sound that infected everything and especially the music. The sound of the train itself was like syncopated breathing, a fast country double-time.

The tambourine ticked off like a piston, and the brushes licked the snare like a breathless hound dog as Jerry Garcia, Janis, Marmaduke and a choir of alcoholic harmonies wailed into "I've Just Seen a Face," stretching out the country, pulling the words apart like a rubber band, "I'm fah-ling, yes, I'm faaaah-lll-iing . . ." and when they got to the end they just started again. "This is one of those endless songs," Bob Weir said. "If I could remember how it began, maybe we could find an ending or we could just go on singing this all night."

Eventually the song dribbled off, and everybody started singing with heavy emphasis John's melancholy imitation of Dylan, which because of some internal structure of its own became the ultimate Beatles Beach Party song. While everybody else was nailing down the chorus *"Heeey! You've got to hide your lovaway . . ."* with alcoholic dexterity, Janis was moving about the lounge giving a soul lecture in a sort of counterpoint gospel: "Li-i-isten, honey, ya can't put your love out on the street, no, no, no, no, nooooh, you've got to put your love in a pot, honey 'n' take it on home . . ." The effect of all this was beautiful and ecstatic despite the fact that the harmonies had collapsed completely, and the voices squealed and whined trying to reach the high notes.

The whole party looks and sounds like Merle Haggard live at Independence Hall on the 4th of July gone completely crazy: Clark Pierson wearing a Mickey Mouse T-shirt and calling out for a barmaid, Roosevelt wearing a beige-and-red striped jump suit styled after a pair of coveralls, Geri, a star of the Warhol movie *Trash,* in a fringed green suede vest and nothing else, like an exploding green pepper, and Charlebois' Cajun fiddler Philippe Gugnon wearing his gray stovepipe hat. His long lean face made him look like an Ozark Lincoln.

"Hey, is that my guitar, man?" asked Janis, sitting cross-legged on an amp in her 30's hustler dress slit up to her thighs. Covered with beads, in her $4.95 hooker shoes, her cigarette holder, feathers, and the Stars and Stripes wrapped around her neck like a scarf, she looked like the personification of a national holiday being celebrated by a display of fireworks.

Someone handed Janis her Gibson Hummingbird. "I only know one song, honey, but I'm gonna sing it anyhow." And Janis began singing "Bobby McGee" with her incredible intensity so that it no longer sounded like Kristofferson's vaguely country folk song, but more like a gospel blues, while Jerry Garcia picked out sweet steel guitar licks that danced around Janis's raunchy voice. Everyone joined in on the chorus; it was like the national anthem of the Festival Express and it must have been sung a hundred times on this trip, in bars, backstage, in compartments late at night, in hotel lobbies, and along the tracks. Seemed to sum up everything that everybody went through on this journey:

Busted flat in Baton Rouge and headin' for the trains
Feeling nearly faded as my jeans
Bobby thumbed a diesel down just before it rained
Took us all away to New Orleans.

I took my harpoon out of my dirty red bandana
And was blowin' sad while Bobby sang the blues
With them windshield wipers slappin' time and Bobby
　　clappin' hands
We finally sang up every song that driver knew.

Freedom's just another word for nothin' left to lose
Nothin' ain't worth nothin' but it's free
Feeling good was easy Lord when Bobby sang the blues
Feeling good was good enough for me,
Good enough for me and Bobby McGee.
　　　　　　—Kris Kristofferson and Fred Foster,
　　　　　　"Bobby McGee," *Combine Music Corp.*

The Cajun fiddler with his chrome-plate violin was trying to play along, but he couldn't find the key. "Play the mother fucker. I'll back you," Jerry told him, and he began one of his backwoods reels, tapping out an incredible patter with his feet on an old suitcase to keep time. "Hey, this guy plays with his feet, man," Janis said.

"Bon finis, bon finis!" Janis applauded, as he finished his number. The fiddler beamed. He asked her to dance, and they twirled around for a couple of reels like two imaginary creatures from Edward Lear, dancing wildly by the light of the moon, and then in a sentimental moment he played "You Are My Sunshine," and his heart was in his bow.

Yodels and coyote calls ring around the lounge as he saws away like a fiddler at a barn dance. Sam Cutler charges through this impromptu hoedown with the totemic gallon-sized bottle of whiskey, like a screeching Redskin from Rimbaud's new-star-infused and milky sea poem "The Drunken Train." He does a do-si-do around the floor and flies off into the inner reaches of the train.

John Barleycorn was king here, and Janis was cackling triumphantly. Finally got the Dead drunk! No one was immune from the deluge of spirits. The CNR cop was playing the tambourine, and at every lull in the music he shouted out a request for "Holy, Holly" by Neil Diamond. It fell on deaf ears. Someone offered him a joint. He walked over, looking like he was actually going to take it.

"I just wanted to smell it," he said sheepishly.

It was the last night on the train, and everybody was aware of it. "Let's just refuse to leave!" Jerry Garcia suggested. A number of impossible suggestions were made, like diverting the train to San Francisco. "We could have the whole goddam city turn out to meet us at the Union Station," John Cooke said.

Talk of home, and everybody starts getting nostalgic. Freewheelin' Frank, and Janis's dog George, Gypsy Boots candy bars, the ocean, movies on the late show, giant beds with silk sheets, and all the minute familiars. Eric Andersen and Janis are singing a Hank Williams song softly over the hum, and its plaintive words drift in and out of the conversations like a sigh.

> Hear the lonesome whippoorwill
> He sounds too blue to fly
> The midnight train is whining low
> I'm so lonesome I could cry.
> —Hank Williams,
> *Fred Rose Music*

Things ended on a comic note, however— Rick Danko singing in his hokey country voice, as creaky as Chester in *Gunsmoke*.

"I been in jail, and I got a jail sentence for 99 years."

"Oh, no, not 99 years to wear the ball and chain?" someone asked incredulously.

"Yeah," said Rick, continuing the story. "So my old lady came to visit me, and she said, 'Son, but you don't have to think about this, because, because it's the best of the tears,' and we all said:

" 'Ooh, ooh, ooh,
And we all said,
No more cane in the Brazos.' "

RICK: So I said, "Captain, don't you do me like you done me . . ." And the words became more surrealistic, stumbling over one another in their eagerness to finish the line. The evening ended with a hymn, "Amazing Grace," and a thundering version of "Goodnight Irene" that was so loud it seemed as if it would rock the train right off the tracks.

The Soup and the Clouds

MANY MUSICIANS ended their day with breakfast and started with late lunch or dinner, straggling into the dining car for the last call. It was one of the few occasions when sober, unstoned dialogues took place. The first meal of the day generally brought out the passengers' reveries. "I could just lie in my bed for hours, watching the trees and rivers go by," said Eric Andersen, "and letting collected memories drop on my head. It's only when you're drunk or happy that you have the courage to remember, and I just get delirious watching all this go by . . . silver, singing skies."

Tom Rush, in his snakeskin jacket, pointed out a lush green valley furling out of a lazy river on the right; someone else saw a cloud in the shape of a giant's toe. But Sam Cutler, like the jaded pirate he is, caustically denounced these romantic yearnings with a loud bellowing "I've already got over the *trees!*"

For those who found it difficult to get themselves together after an all-night session, Janis always had some good advice. To a tomato-juice-drinking neighbor she suggested, screwdriver in hand, "When you're out of vodka, just go on and use some gin in the juice, honey. Really, it's the way to do it. Just don't smell the gin."

There was no caboose at the end of the train, but after a late lunch you *could* sit on the little platform at the end of the last car and watch the tracks taper into the vanishing point. Although northern Ontario seemed to be an uninhabited landscape from this unobstructed viewpoint, one could see elk, rabbits, moose, and the occasional human. Jerry Garcia reported seeing a large black bear scratching its back on a birch tree.

Duck hunters in an aluminum boat flash by on our right, a family on an outing in the middle of a field are frozen instamatically as the train rushes past. At night the wandering polestar, which is called the "Nail of the Sky" by Buriat Shamans, crawls across the universe like an incandescent bug as the train wiggles through the forest.

It was at one of these late breakfasts, hung up between eating and seeing, that an unexpected friendship began, a product of the train's cosmic calculus, and as fateful as any chance encounter on the Orient Express. And, after all, as Janis observed, "Chance is just the fool's name for fate."

When I entered the dining car that afternoon, I saw Janis and Bonnie talking animatedly over a late breakfast. I was curious, and I thought to myself a little guiltily that I would definitely like to overhear what was going down. But it was hard to find a place in the crowded car, and so the only alternative was just to walk over to the table and hang out, which is just what I did not do. My nerve failed me. To begin with, I was a little in awe of Bonnie's raunchy style, different from Janis's but formidable, and I sat down, resigned to never hearing their conversation.

A minute later, I looked up, my spoon in a lake, to see Janis in a trance. "Hey, man, what kind of a fuckin writer are you?" she asked in her amazing, rusty voice. "Bonnie and I are having this incredible rap, and you're missing the whole thing, man."

"It's a private conversation, Janis . . ."

"Don't give me any of that apologetic shit,

man. Where's your tape recorder? You've gotta get this down, it's just gotta be one of the most far-out conversations that ever took place. This chick is really beautiful, man, she's as fuckin macho as me. Can you believe that? Private, my ass, man. This is *your* gig, honey. You're meant to be *working,* getting your shit together, man. You're not here to have a good time, I mean, this ain't just a fuckin party, man, you know!"

Janis's attitudes about work and obligations struck me at first as weird and out of character, but it was a very real part of her personality, and after a while I began to relish the incongruity of her careening wild self, suddenly turning into this almost righteous Victorian matron, denouncing sloth, carelessness, stupidity, and infirmity of purpose with evangelistic zeal. Everybody had their work cut out for them in this world, and as indulgent as Janis was, she felt it was a blasphemy to cop out, fall down on a job, not get it together, or let something fall apart out of incompetence. It was almost as if all minute particulars of this inequity were crucial to the way things happened in the Kozmos. *Jesus Christ, we let the Garden of Eden get away once already. We aren't going to let it happen again, are we, boys?*

Although the source of much of this was obviously her Republican upbringing and the absorption of her parents into her system, in Janis these pieces had transformed themselves to the level of myth. It was the sort of nostalgia for paradise vividly present in archaic peoples where all these lapses are blurs of grace: slipping from a branch of the Kozmic Tree, tripping at the foot of the ladder, falling asleep, losing one's way. Original sin in every fault in endless repetition. "Hey, man, you don't have to keep reminding me that we blew it!"

Janis was definitely an authority on this state of things, otherwise known as the Kozmic Blues. Fortunately, there are certain chosen individuals who can set things back the way they were, and Janis knew she was one of them. The spell is temporary and evaporates with doubt. But the price of this power is always pain, and Janis lived in intimacy with pain. All her bawdy accents, liquid humor, and displays of courage could not shout it down. In understanding that it is the sum of petty accidents that have sewn us into our dilemma Janis guessed that *rightly to be great is to find quarrel in a straw.*

Symbolic Wounds

IN THE reflective present I return with the tape recorder, and soon all these moments about to be are coded, set forever in this amber electric pool; retrievable but irreversible, the sentences proceeding into the inevitable, like Pantagruel's sailing accidentally into a sea of frozen sounds.

THEN HE threw on the deck before us whole handfuls of frozen words, which looked like crystalized sweets of different colors. We saw some words gules, or gay quips, some vert, some azure, some sable, and some or. When we warmed them a little between our hands, they melted like snow, and we actually heard them, though we did not understand them, for they were in a barbarous language. There was one exception, however, a fairly big one. This, when Friar John picked it up, made a noise like a chestnut that has been thrown on the embers without being pricked. It was an explosion, and made us all start with fear. "That," said Friar John, "was a cannon shot in its day."
　　　　　　　　　—Rabelais, *Gargantua and Pantagruel*

We move from the dining room into the bar car. Janis seems to float through the passageways, a blur of colors and textures: feathers, velvet, satin, purple, blue, magenta. Tie-dyed passages like white moss leech into purple plains and magenta fur. Her boas hug each other in bright ice-cream colors, and every slight gesture or movement shudders this heady azure-cobalt vegetation into little pools of red and blue, as if a breath of wind had picked up somewhere between her wrist and her elbow and brushed its way among the leaves and tendrils of this unlikely garden. Here, *ripeness is all.* Outside, the sad, flat, interminable honey-colored plains look apologetic and resentful in comparison. But nature at this latitude was little competition for Janis, and, anyway her landscapes were always more fluorescent than organic. Neon petals, blots, and blurs, flashy crystal weeds that sprang up in the harsh phosphorescent light of honky-tonks and bars. Tough-hooker threads, metallic gaudy baubles, tawdry, exaggerated, digging themselves, talking back at sneaky glances . . . "Dig my shit, baby" . . . "Uh, hiya there, honey . . . whatch'all doin tonight?" Sultry Mother Earth, her eyes on stalks, sees Janis through the window of the train and rushes off wildly to the right and left.

At the core of all this efflorescence, Janis herself, like a four o'clock flower gradually unfolding, as the afternoon revolves around her in the tiny bar car, a rustic Victoria in her most carnal aspect. Strangely, all the gaudy bangles, tacky jewelry, hooker shoes, cannot conceal her matronly regality, a curiously gothic fertility figure attended by tiny devotional sounds: ice tinkling brittlely against glass, mournful as dry salvage, bells, orders, muffled hums of peripheral conversation, and from the next car a low whining guitar drifts monotonously, circling in endless lazy spirals as if fixing on a still point at the center of the music.

Bonnie slouches in her chair as casually as Huck on his raft. Pretty tomboy looks in Levi's and a peasant shirt. Plaintive earnest, making wry faces at plates of the past she serves up to herself almost accidentally. The sad times seem to fly after her and Janis in this half-submerged alcoholic state. But they extricate themselves swiftly in sudden torrents of laughter. Janis's unmetrical laugh that seems to lead its own robust existence deep inside her arrives on the spur of the moment, a wild rampaging guffaw galloping to rescue an endangered flank. But no sooner have they risen above one sinking moment than they alight carelessly upon another only to discover their resting place is infested with other memories scarcely less treacherous. Two ballsy chicks railing against the unfairness of things, women is losers, ball and chain . . . but what they have more in common than their brittle street rap is the depth of their vulnerability and sensitivity barely covered by the cheap vinyl defenses that they have wrapped around themselves. Tough, but melting easily, quizzical, petty, resentful of a host of wrongs and hurts both trivial and intimate, unexpectedly profound as well as ready to pawn off clichés on each other, slipping imperceptibly from state to state . . .

Bonnie whines and pleads with her own histories, extorting apologies from invisible defendants, and turns unexpectedly to tell a tale as poignant and innocent as Giulietta Massina in *La Strada*: When she was a child growing up in the South, her mother took her to see this black gospel singer at a little club in her home town. She was mesmerized, unable to move as the witness of a vision. She asked her mother if she could go up to the man and touch him. As she put her tiny hand on his arm he turned and looked at her. And from that day on she felt possessed. The only solace she could find was to take the demon back to its source: to sing.

JANIS [*to waiter*]: Screwdriver.
BONNIE: Scotch and Coke.
JANIS: I've got lots of tie-dyed velvet . . . I had these tie-dyed satin sheets, the most beautiful fuckin sheets in the world and I started makin it with this cowboy and he shredded them up with his cowboy boots.

[*Laughs, ice tinkling.*] Three-hundred-dollar satin sheets shredded by cowboy boots. I loved every minute of it.
BONNIE: Is that true?
JANIS: It is true, man, they're ruined.
BONNIE: Now, that dude can't've been that good.
JANIS [*Cracks up*]: Well, how do you see it so far, David?
DAVID: It's a gas.
JANIS: So do I. To tell you the truth, man, I've woken up a lot . . . Listen, I didn't take this gig . . . the money ainthat great . . . I didn't take this gig for any reason other than this party, man. . . . I said it sounds like a party, man and I wanta be there . . . my band are picking us up in Winnipeg, and the Band are picking us up in Winnipeg . . . and I'm gonna pick one of them up in Winnipeg!
BONNIE: Hey, did you see our organ player? His name is Jim Gordon. And, Janis I swear to God, Rick and Robbie were there . . . for ten years I worked with him . . . [*catches a look on Janis's face*] . . . oh yeah . . . you read that article, huh? [*Janis cackles*] I knew you'd read it, I read it too . . .
JANIS: The chick's beautiful, man . . . how old are you? What sign are you?
BONNIE: I'm 25.
JANIS: Gosh, you're younger than me.
BONNIE: You're 27, right?
JANIS: You seem as old as me.
BONNIE: I am as old as you. I'm older than you.
JANIS: I've been on the streets ten years.
BONNIE: *I've* been on the street ten years. You ain't got that on me, I've been there too.
JANIS: I knew you looked good. You just fired your old band, didn't you?
BONNIE: No, our old band just quit. They wanted to pick with Joe Cocker.
JANIS: All those 87 people? When I saw Joe Cocker at the Fillmore West and I read

in *Rolling Stone* he had an 87-piece group, children, dogs, chicks, musicians, and he brings all life onto the stage, I went down to the Fillmore, and Bill Graham didn't let no one on the stage but the musicians—he made all the chicks, all the babies, all the dogs, stand on the side, because if he's singing and if he's playing music, he's playing music. He ain't talking about a life style, he ain't philosophizing, he's playing music, and he ought to get musicians up there and play the shit, man, if he wants groupies he can get 'em after the show.

BONNIE: You can get them local, man, you don't have to bring them. My girl friend told me that she got in a fight with her girl friend because her girl friend said that she read in *Rolling Stone* that someone was supposed to have seen me yelling to them, "You dirty mother fuckers, you stole my band," and all this shit, and it made me really mad because I really love my musicians.

JANIS: Did you lose that great organ player?

BONNIE: Bobby Whitlock, man, he's in England with Eric. There's a million and one musicians in this world that's never even been heard of that can just kick ass.

JANIS: Yeah, playing topless clubs and things.

BONNIE: Yeah, so as far as your musical ability, we can always find other musicians, but I love those guys and it really did crush me, but I was cool, and it hurt me and it killed me, but I was cool. And it's a lie that I said it; it may not be a lie what I thought. I was crushed, I can admit it now we have a new band, we're together. In the meantime, you know Bobby Keys: that great sax player had no gigs, man, because they let him down. Eric told him he could come over to England and make a lot of bread doing sessions and he believed him, so now he says he can't pay for the plane, so in the meantime he's sitting home with no gigs, because I'm not going to fire the new band.

JANIS: I've worked with three bands, four including when I was a kid, but three pro bands. We got on stage and did it anyway under the lights, but those boys really help you. The singer is only as good as the band, and this is the first band that really helped me. I got a drummer, man that drives me up a wall. I wanna tell you, I was doing this shit in a tune last week, you know how you have verse, bridge, verse, and then you have a vamp. The vamp is free, it's Janis, Janis gets to sing or talk or walk around the stage and act foxy, whatever she wants to do, right. It's free, and all the band is supposed to do is keep up the groove. So I was singing, "Well I told that man, I said baby, I said baby, I said baby," I went up in thirds, and when I hit that high "baby" and I did a kick with my ass to the right, and the drummer went bam! with a rim shot, and I turned around and said "My God, where did you learn that part, man, I just made it up a minute ago." I walked off stage and said, "Where did you learn to play behind singers like that?" and he said, "I used to back strippers." That's how you learn how to play, man.

BONNIE: Watch that ass, when it's going to the right you hit a rim shot. That's exactly what I tell my drummer.

DAVID: Clark is a great drummer.

JANIS: He's not subtle, but he's all right. Right on. I guess that's what I need. I ain't real subtle either, to tell the truth.

BONNIE: When you listen to your band, what do you listen to the most?

JANIS: Drums and bass.

BONNIE: I know this, me too, drums and bass. It's the bottom, it's the rhythm.

JANIS: That's what kicks you.

BONNIE: Since you are a lead instrument yourself. Everyone wants to play their own ax, like the greatest guitar player. You listen immediately to the bottom, so you're the lead instrument, so all you need is rhythm.

JANIS: All you need is the bottom, the middle you just count on to fill in, but what you need is that kick in your ass, man.

BONNIE: Because you know you're gonna do your lead right as long as your bass and drummer are together.

JANIS: If you get the kick in the ass. You hear it when they're great. But mostly I'm so involved with the song that I don't even hear the band, you know what I mean? All I hear is when they're wrong. When they're right, I just keep singing and talking my shit and telling my stories, but as soon as someone does something wrong, man, I get goony.

BONNIE: When you're rapping and all of a sudden they hit a hum, dum, dum, into another groove, and you ain't ready for it, you turn around and look at that drummer and bass player. Jim Keltner used to get so mad at me, he'd say, "Why do you turn around and give me dirty looks?" That's no dirty look, that's my face.

JANIS: That's when you were in the wrong place when I was in the other place.

BONNIE: I was here and you were there, and you're not supposed to be nowhere that I ain't.

JANIS: That's what I dig about the group I got now. I had groups that learned the tunes, they learned the stops, they learned the whatever-the-fuck. This band, man, I could be in the middle of a verse and go on a different trip, and they can follow me. They won't go with the arrangement, they go right with me, man. Like if I decide to extend the verse for 8 bars, 16 bars, whatever the bars are called, when I get through saying something I ain't through so I keep talkin, they don't quit, they know I'm not through so they keep playing.

BONNIE: I used to do the exact same thing with Delaney, I'd never keep my eyes off

him, because you never know what he's gonna do—he might want to tell his life story.

JANIS: I do it all the time.

BONNIE: I do it too, I tell my life story every show I do.

JANIS: Sometimes I wonder if they're worth it, man, if they're worth all that fuckin grief that they drag out of you, but you can't think about it in those terms, right?

BONNIE: The only thing I wonder about is not if they're worth it but if they understand it, because I hate to expose myself completely and have it go this far over their heads. Because that's what you're doing, you're taking off completely the whole plastic down from the front of you, you might as well just get nude. Because you're completely exposing your inside feelings. It's reality, it's not a show when you really get into it as much as that. I really get uptight, not at what they yell, it's just that they shouldn't yell anything at all. What I want to hear from that audience is understanding, I don't want to hear someone yell "Where's Clapton?" I'm standin up there, I got 3 children and it's very hard to go off and leave them, that's part of me, and I'm not saying it. I'm giving up someone who really belongs to me, because this is something I have to do as a complete individual, but they are individuals, too, so I can't subject them to my life; it's their own choice, I don't get them high, I don't get high in front of them, I don't want to give them mescaline, that's their own choice. I wish I could take that tape from Germany, because we never played so hot, and they were yelling, boo, hiss, they yelled from the minute we hit that stage with Eric, because they figured Eric was going to have his own shit. Eric Clapton with Delaney and Bonnie and Friends, it looks like there's Eric Clapton's group and then Delaney and Bonnie, they didn't think he was going to play with us. I have no pride. It hurt my feelings, I cried, and I couldn't do any more than four numbers, because I'm not going to cram anything down anyone's throat who don't dig it. You're completely putting the whole plastic shield down and exposing your whole inner feelings to everyone. This is the only way I can get release from what I feel, you gotta talk, you gotta tell, and I have the God-given talent to be able to do that, I don't have to live in a plastic shell all my life, and I think it should be appreciated, and if you don't like it, I think you should get your money and split, and if people writing about it don't dig it, they have no business interviewing me, let them interview someone they like, because if you don't have something nice to say, don't write about that person.

JANIS: I had a couple of shows where I played the whole show really into it, completely giving all I had, man, and I was doing a free-form thing, talking, bring it all out, let it all go, man. Just talked about Janis and all the men that hurt her, and all the men that maybe she let down, and everything that you got to say, man, all of a sudden it starts coming out of your mouth, and you didn't even intend it to, and all of a sudden I heard them speak, I heard them talkin in the middle of my fuckin shit, man, and I stopped and I waited to see if they'd quit.

BONNIE: It's like a sledgehammer in your chest, man.

JANIS: They didn't quit, and I grabbed the microphone and said, I ain't cryin my ass for you, man. I put the microphone down and walked off the stage. I blew my contract and all that shit, but fuck that, man, I ain't gonna get out there and cry my soul out for people that are talking about "How's your brother, did you get laid on Thursday, that's a cute dress." I'm up there talking about my pain, fuck you, man.

BONNIE: Our pain is common. You know the feeling that a woman has—it's very hard for a man to get to a woman because they take it in different ways. It's like a woman can understand another woman, and everyone has been in love and been turned down and everyone has had someone who really loved them that they just didn't love, and what are you going to do, you don't want to hurt him, but you just don't love him, and that's hurt and that's pain. So you're telling that to people, and there's a lot of people that can relate to that. In the meantime Joe Shmoe is assin off, and you're being very serious, and people say, "Delaney walked off stage, he thinks he's so hot." He's exposing himself, and everyone's laughing, they're ignoring him, ignoring his whole soul. It's really ugly to do, because everyone in the meantime is talking about understanding and loving one another, and peace, and let's talk about it, let's be truthful with each other. And here's someone on a platform in front of thousands of people, there's probably 45,000 that understand, that have been through that, and then there's the others that have maybe been through that but don't even want to look at it, so they want to schmaltz it up for everyone else. And if it so happens that they're sitting in the front row, and you're trying to do something, if you were Frank Sinatra you could look up to the left light or the right light, but I gotta look my people in the eye.

JANIS: That's what's so hard.

BONNIE: Why did they spend their money to come there?

JANIS: It's the 50's against the 60's. In the 50's they used to sing songs because they had nice tunes and they had nice melodies, they didn't hear the words. They were nice to fox-trot to or something. Right now, it's different for a guitar player because he's playing D minor, F, whatever the fuck, but I'm up there saying, "I feel, you know, I hurt, please help," I'm saying words, man, and if I look at an audience, and they ain't understanding me, it's just like getting kicked in the teeth.

BONNIE: As much money as Las Vegas has they ain't got enough for me, they gonna have to come up with a lot of bread.

JANIS: I turned them down, too. Do you know what's very strange, bizarre? Seven or 8 years from now the people going to Las Vegas will be fans of ours, they're gonna have grown up, and they're gonna be going to Las Vegas. In ten years, honey, it's gonna be our crowd, man, we can go back there and rock and roll. The 60's are selling now in Las Vegas, in ten years from now the 70's are gonna be selling, and if the Jefferson Airplane still manage to keep their dregs together, they're gonna be playing there, too.

BONNIE: I certainly hope you're right, man, because I had a super bummer in Las Vegas.

JANIS: I went there once, I checked into this motel and they gave me a coupon worth a dollar at the roulette table, a dollar in quarters at the slot machine, and a coupon worth two drinks. I played a dollar's worth of roulette and I lost, I played a dollar's worth of slot machines and I lost, I had two free drinks and said "Fuck 'em." I came out of there stoned anyway. They ask me, "How did you learn how to sing like that, how did you learn how to sing the blues, how did you learn how to sing that heavy?" I didn't learn shit, man, I just opened my mouth and that's what I sounded like, man. You can't make up something that you don't feel. Bonnie, she's a bitchin singer, you know she ain't making up nothing, that chick's a woman, man. I don't know what kind of dues she's paying, but she's paid them, she's still paying them. She's an honest to God real-life woman, man, or she wouldn't be able to sound like that. I didn't make it up, I just opened my mouth, and it existed.

BONNIE: You know that a lot of people say the trouble with women is they don't think about what they say before they say it.

JANIS: That's the good thing about women, man. Because they sing they fuckin insides, man. Women to be in the music business give up more than you'd ever know. She's got kids she gave up, any woman gives up home life, an old man, probably, you give up a home and friends, children and friends, you give up an old man and friends, you give up every constant in the world except music. That's the only thing in the world you got, man. So for a woman to sing, she really needs to or wants to. A man can do it as a gig, because he knows he can get laid tonight.

BONNIE: A lot of musicians are married and worship the footsteps their wives walk in, but they go on the road, and they ball, and they have a ball, but when they are home no one is going to break their marriage up, there ain't nobody gonna hurt their children. But what man would have you and let you do what you must do?

JANIS: That's the trouble, you either got to be as big a star as the chick or you got to be a flunky, and no woman, at least me, I don't want an ass-kisser, I want a cat that's bigger and stronger and ballsier than me. When I'm pulling my shit as a singer it's hard to find him, because the only cats that hang around dressing rooms are flunkies. They're all right for a night, but when you want to talk about a man, ain't no man in the world needs to hang around a dressing room. The men are out in some log cabin growing grass and chopping trees, and I never get to see them. But that gives you more soul, right?

BONNIE: When Delaney and I met, it was that fast, I married him seven days after I met him. I was never married before, I was 23, he was never married and 26, and no one even thought about getting married. For ten years before I met Delaney I lived in hell. I worked in strip joints and truck stops and I went on between the second-best and the best stripper—you got to have a break so the star could come out—I'd be up there singing a song and they be yelling, "Take it off, baby!"

JANIS: I wasn't even a chick singer until I became a chick singer. I was a dope dealer and a hanging-out artist and a chick on the street trying to find a place to sleep and a cat to lay. I didn't ever sing until they turned me into a rock and roll singer. I sang for free beer once in a while, but I never even wanted to grow up to be a singer, it was a very bizarre experience.

BONNIE: It's really weird, I never wanted to be anything else, that was my whole life.

JANIS: All my life I just wanted to be a beatnik, meet all the heavies, get stoned, get laid, have a good time, that's all I ever wanted, except I knew I had a good voice and I could always get a couple of beers off of it. All of a sudden someone threw me in this rock and roll band. They threw these musicians at me, man, and the sound was coming from behind, the bass was charging me, and I decided then and there that that was it, I never wanted to do anything else. It was better than it had been with any man, you know. Maybe that's the trouble. . . .

PHOTOGRAPHS

''Have a seat,'' said Janis, gesturing across the table. ''Let's see what you've got.'' She was having a drink and was getting loose—a caricature of ''Rock Super Queen Bee at Home.''

Watching her at close range confirmed something that had always puzzled me about her pictures. No two pictures of her ever looked the same, and now I could see why. Not only was her normal, conversational face dynamic and constantly changing, but even statically she just *looked* completely different from any new angle. Some people have certain features which dominate their appearance from any perspective, but Janis had a face in which each feature took its turn. Straight on, you might notice her eyes only. At three-quarter view her nose took over, and at full profile her chin forced you to reassess her eyes and nose in terms of a new geometry— Hooded eyes becoming gaunt and the broad nose becoming almost beaked.

Even her complexion changed with the angle of incident light, changing from conspicuously rough to inconspicuously smooth with the tosses of her head, at which time her hair might fall into any one of a dozen unrelated configurations. I started to understand analytically what all of these girls understood intuitively. Janis was the composite of them all.

—Bruce Steinberg in a letter.

San Jose, 1968 (JEFFREY BLANKFORT/BBM)

Overleaf: San Jose, 1968 (JIM MARSHALL)

San Jose, 1968 (JEFFREY BLANKFORT/BBM)

Monterey Pop Festival, 1967 (DAVID DALTON)

Overleaf: Panhandle Park, San Francisco, 1966 (JIM MARSHALL)

With Pigpen, San Jose, 1968 (JEFFREY BLANKFORT/BBM)

Golden Gate Park, 1966 (JIM MARSHALL)

San Jose, 1968 (JEFFREY BLANKFORT/BBM)

Chelsea Hotel, 1970 (DAVID GAHR)
Overleaf: Big Brother Rehearsal Loft, 1967 (JIM MARSHALL)

Above: with Bill Graham. *Below:* with Freewheelin Frank (JIM MARSHALL)

Above: with Grace Slick. *Below:* with Country Joe MacDonald (JIM MARSHALL)

With R. Crumb. Opening of New Comix Show, Berkeley, 1969 (ELIHU BLOTNICK/BBM)

With Michael J. Pollard (JOHN FISHER)
Overleaf: Backstage, Winterland, 1967 (JIM MARSHALL)

Above: Home, Port Arthur, Texas, 1970 (JOHN FISHER). *Below:* with Mr. Threadgill (DAVID GAHR)

Above: with Onward Brass Band, Newport, 1968 (DAVID GAHR). *Below:* last performance, Capitol Theatre, 1970 (JOHN FISHER)

Backstage, Winterland, 1968 (JIM MARSHALL)

Madison Square Garden, 1969 (CHRIS WOLF)

Madison Square Garden, 1969 (ROBERT ALTMAN)

Overleaf (JIM MARSHALL)

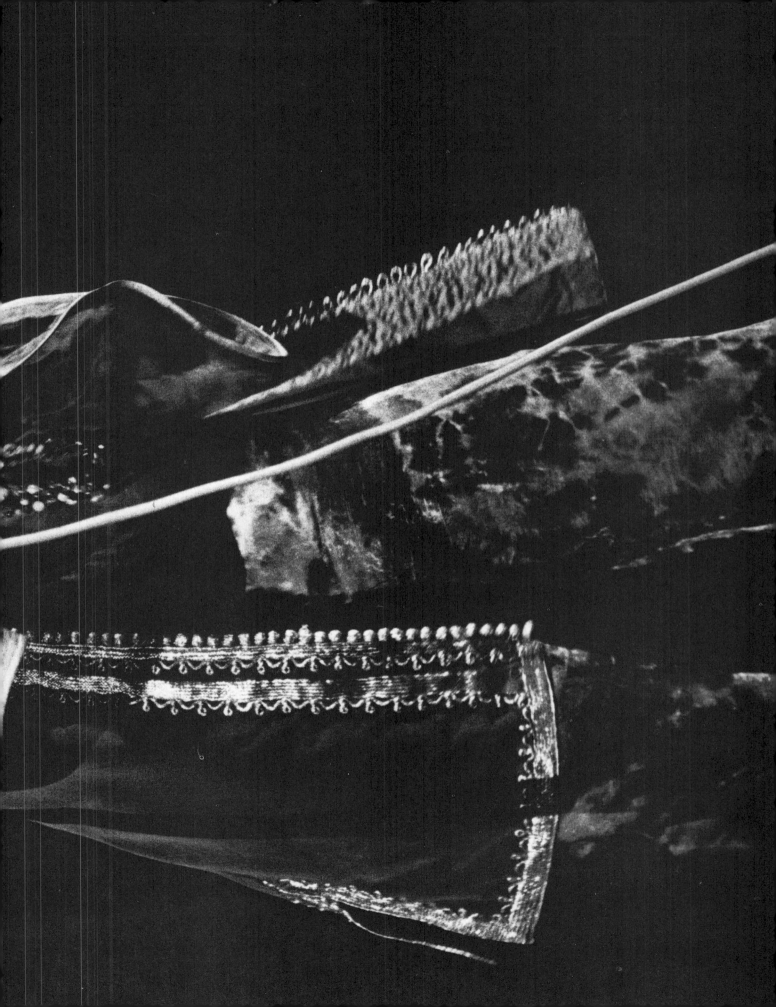

Above, right, and overleaf: Newport Folk Festival, 1968 (DAVID GAHR)

Overleaf: Fillmore West, 1968 (JIM MARSHALL)　　　　　　　　*Above:* Chelsea Hotel, 1970 (DAVID GAHR

Chelsea Hotel, 1970 (DAVID GAHR)

Overleafs: New York, 1970 (DAVID GAHR)

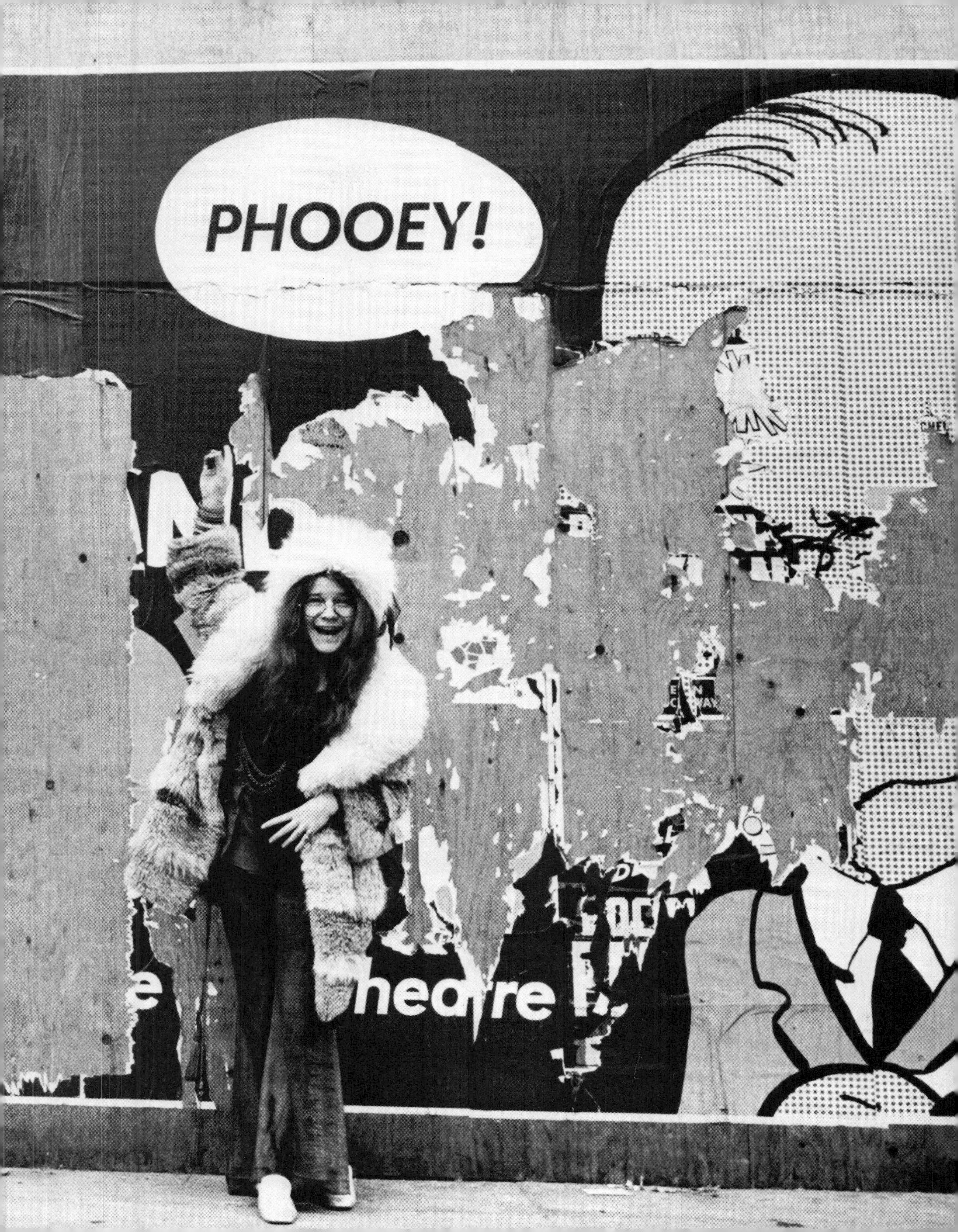
PHOOEY!
heatre

Above and left: Roof of Chelsea Hotel, 1970 (DAVID GAHR)   *Overleaf:* Winterland, 1968 (JIM MARSHALL)

Outside Albert Hall, London, 1969 (RICHARD DILELLO)

FUGITIVE PIECES

(Excerpts from *Rolling Stone*)

21   And the Lord said, Behold, there is a place
by me, and thou shalt stand upon a rock:
22   And it shall come to pass, while my glory
passeth by, that I will put thee in a cleft of the
rock, and will cover thee with my hand while I
pass by:
23   And I will take away mine hand, and thou
shalt see my back parts: but my face shall not
be seen.

—*Exod.* 33:21–23

PART SIX

FUGITIVE PIECES

It was at the Monterey Pop Festival in 1967 that Janis's career and the idea for Rolling Stone *were first set in motion. Monterey gave Janis her first major exposure, and it was as a result of the festival that Jann Wenner decided to put together* Rolling Stone. *It is ironic, therefore, that Janis and* Rolling Stone *should ultimately have drifted so far apart.*

Hadn't their relationship begun as a heady infatuation with Rolling Stone's *first real mention of Janis? "We see Big Brother in Flashes throughout the intro tune," wrote Al Kooper in his preview of* Monterey Pop, *"but for the most part, the camera's balling Janis. It literally kisses her feet when it displays her unique footwork and moons around that face while she energetically turns on 10,000 people on a Saturday afternoon."*

Janis did not accept criticism lightly, and when the heavy criticism came, she was totally unforgiving. Some of the critical pieces on Janis in Rolling Stone *seem now almost harmless and at the most merely petty, but Janis found it hard to forgive old wounds nevertheless. If her furious attack on* Rolling Stone *which follows seems somewhat out of proportion, it must be said that to Janis any criticism was a personal attack because for her* nothing *was impersonal.*

Listen, *Rolling Stone* were really *always* down on us all the way through Big Brother, they never ever said a decent word about us except they're [*sarcastically*] "well liked" but . . . They talk about how James couldn't play the guitar and how I couldn't sing— they were just always negative, always negative, always negative. And when I went on my own, they like crucified me, man. I really cried behind that, man—they put my picture on the cover, and inside they didn't say it was a bad show or it was a bad band— they said I didn't have it, I wasn't gonna get it, I needed Big Brother—and Ralph Gleason said this and I'll never forgive him—he said I should go back with Big Brother *if they will have me.* You know, cunt shit, cunt shit, bitchy-chick shit, she's-gettin-too-big-for-her-britches shit. They slapped me down, man, they really hurt me, and I know it isn't important what someone says about you, but fuck them, man. I kept on trying, but it still hurts. You know, every time you get laughed at on the street, even though you know the guy's a *dummy,* you still kind of go "a-a-oh-oh," a little bit. Nobody wants to be disliked, man—it's a human failing. But I don't know why they went that far, because it wasn't just commentary, it was vicious, it was really vicious, and that's why I treated you in London like that. They did the same thing to me in Memphis.

What happened was this—we had only been together about a week and a half or two weeks, and we were still pushing—we weren't grooving together yet, we were shaky. Number 1, it's Memphis. Number 2, we're a white hippie group, and number 3, everybody did all those dance steps and shit, and our thing is selling sincerity, and they aren't buying it down there, and also it was a very cold audience. It was a terrible audience, and I don't know why, but I came on very struck, scared, scared to death. But then I watched Johnnie Taylor close the show—the star, Johnnie Taylor—and that's when "Who's Making Love" was a hit, and he's Stax-Volt's own, and he was closing the show, man, and they turned on all the lights so everyone could get out to their cars before everybody else did, man, and they were walking out on Johnnie Taylor! They were really dispassionate—they wanted a show. I'm used to playing for people who want to feel what I feel. They don't give a shit about feeling—they just want to see a few dance steps, a nice boogaloo beat, and go home. It's not my crowd.

He left it like we were really fucked, wrong, out of tune, incapable untalented bores, man. Maybe *Rolling Stone* is too big a business now, but I know at the time what struck me was they knew I was shaky, I didn't know how to put together a group, I never put together a group before, I'd only been in a group with friends, never professional musicians. I didn't know any of that shit, man. They're from San Francisco, I'm from San Francisco, they came out of the same rock culture I came out of, you know if the Grateful Dead needs an amplifier, I'll give them an amplifier. These are my people, I'm one of their people, we're all in the same fight together, and I thought they shot me down when they should have boosted me up— I expected a little help from my friends.

But people don't want to read that.

I know that, that's like saying I can't invite all my friends to my concert free, I gotta sell something or I can't afford to pay everybody. But I really expected a little encouragement from them. I knew I wasn't as great as I was at Monterey—I was doing something I'd never done before—but that's not the time to kick somebody, when they're down. Maybe even a little affirmative criticism—I expected a little help, and I got a kick in the teeth, man. That must give Jann Wenner a great sense of power, to be able to hurt people like that—I wouldn't want to grow up to be like that. Just because he exists doesn't mean he's right, just because he shot down Cream doesn't mean he should've. But I guess there are two ways to look at it—you can say "As a reporter, we felt we had to tell the truth," but *Rolling Stone*'s not all reporting, it's not all facts, it's, you know, "Take it from us, kids, it was like that," and that's so subjective as to approach the ridiculous.

I think you should think in terms of saying something as an entity, using a beginning and ending and middle and climax and the last line and everything to create a character like a novelist.

JANIS
1943–1970

JANIS JOPLIN was born on January 19, 1943, the oldest of three children, in Port Arthur, Texas, a medium-small city of 60,000, located approximately fifteen miles from the Louisiana border. Her father, Seth, was once employed by the Texas Canning Company but now works for Texaco. Her mother, Dorothy, is Registrar at Port Arthur College, a business school. She has a younger sister, Laura, an undergraduate at Lamar Tech in Austin, and a brother, Michael.

Many people in Port Arthur work in the oil refinery business in some capacity, and the city is middle-income and middle-class. It is often smoky and hot. From all reports, Janis hated it.

"In Texas I was a beatnik, a weirdo, and since I wasn't making it the way I am now, my parents thought I was a goner," Janis said in 1968. "Now my mother writes and asks what kind of clothes a 1968 blues singer wears. That's kind of groovy, since we've been on opposite sides since I was fourteen. Texas is OK if you want to settle down and do your own thing quietly, but it's not for outrageous people, and I was always outrageous. I got treated very badly in Texas. They don't treat beatniks too good in Texas."

Her first interests were painting and poetry. She did some of each, but at seventeen, got very involved with Leadbelly country blues and then Bessie Smith. She sent away for albums of both performers, and played them over many times, trying to sing along. Then she ran away.

She stayed in Austin, Houston, Venice Beach and San Francisco, singing and working at various jobs. Sometimes she collected unemployment checks. She is first recorded as being in San Francisco in 1962, but Ken Threadgill, an old-time Texas folk musician, remembers seeing her in Austin in 1961. He claims she'd just been released from a hospital in San Francisco, where she'd been under treatment for drugs. That would place her in California sometime before her nineteenth birthday.

"I first saw her in late '61," Threadgill remembers. "She was just a kid. She came up to Austin to go to school at the University of Texas, and she worked part-time as a keypunch operator to help pay expenses. She was around off and on from '61 to '63."

Threadgill had converted a service station into a bar that featured old-time country music done by young and old performers. Another girl singer, Julie Joyce, who used to work at Threadgill's, saw Janis and a "bluegrass" band she was working parties and occasional coffeehouses with, sitting in the street in Austin. Janis had an autoharp. The other musicians were Powell St. John, a harp player and Larry Wiggins, a banjo picker and guitarist. Julie invited the trio to try out at Threadgill's. In one of her first performances, Janis won two bottles of Lone Star beer. The trio also won a ten-dollar prize in a talent show.

"Actually though, she didn't go over so well around there. She was singing in a high, shrill bluegrass kind of sound. Eventually somebody came around who put her on a coffeehouse circuit and that was that," Threadgill said.

Back in Port Arthur at a party one night, she tried an Odetta imitation and the new sound she was capable of startled even her. She continued to restrain her vocals though, doing Bessie Smith-type songs in bars and folk clubs, right up until the first time she worked out with Big Brother and the Holding Company.

Janis told people she'd been in and out of four colleges over the next years, but she definitely was in San Francisco in 1966. Chet Helms, who was then running a musicians' and rehearsal house in the Haight-Ashbury and managing Big Brother, heard and liked her.

Sam Andrew, Peter Albin, James Gurley and later Dave Getz had been hanging around Chet Helms' pad in Haight-Ashbury in 1965.

"First time I ever met Peter, he had this weird idea for starting a rock group which would speak to all the children of the nation in their own language," Sam said. "I thought, what's this nut trying to do, what trip is he on?" The band began practicing and took the name Big Brother and the Holding Company. They were Helms' house band at the Avalon.

"Before Janis we were doing a lot of space stuff, kind of what Cecil Taylor and Pharaoh Sanders were doing . . . just hard and very free," Sam remembers. At first it was more experimentation. Peter was doing most of the singing, and when Janis came he taught the songs to Janis.

"We wanted another singer; I think maybe one or two people in the group were thinking of Signe and the Airplane and how that worked out. But most of us were thinking of just any vocalist who came along who was good. And Chet was managing us, and he said 'I know this great chick.' Janis had come out to San Francisco before and freaked out—she didn't think she was going anywhere—and she went back to Texas. So Chet went back and told her about the scene, and she and Travis Rivers came out. So we moved to Lagunitas and got into country living, and it was a growing-together thing for all of us. The rest of us were still new to each other and Janis was a catalyst, brought people out, made it really easy to talk."

Janis, in 1968: "[Chet] told me Big Brother was looking for a chick singer, so I thought I'd give it a try. I don't know what happened. I just exploded. I'd never sung like that before. I stood still, and I sang simple. But you *can't* sing like that in front of a rock band, all that rhythm and volume going. You *have* to sing loud and move wild with all that in back of you. It happened the first time, but then I got turned on to Otis Redding, and I just got into it more than ever. Now, I don't know how to perform any other way. I've tried cooling myself and not screaming, and I've walked off feeling like nothing."

Janis and Big Brother—Sam and Jim on guitars, Peter on bass and Dave on drums—worked the Avalon regularly and other small gigs around the Bay area. They were building a reputation with the city's ballroom goers. Janis had moved back to town, and was living in a second floor apartment near Buena Vista Park, in the same block as Peter Albin. Country Joe McDonald of the Fish was going with her for a time. Then Big Brother got an offer to record. The label was Mainstream, a small Chicago outfit, and Sam Andrew still thinks of the incident as a "disaster":

"This cat was pushing us—this really far-out mother from New York. They had an audition at the old Spreckels mansion; they wanted to sign us then, and Chet said no. A couple of months later we got rid of Chet, for one reason or another it didn't make it. Then we went to Chicago and signed, because it sounded so attractive . . . we were naive kids. We were in Chicago and it was heavy; the club was burning us and here was this cat saying come on down to the recording studio tomorrow, sign up and let's go to a lawyer and make sure it's cool—and it was *his* lawyer—I think we all wanted to, more or less.

"We asked him for $1,000, and he said no. We said $500? He said no. Well, can we have plane fare home? He said not one penny, and to this day we haven't got one penny from that album (*Big Brother and the Holding Company*, Mainstream 36099). We got back and it was a good time in San Francisco, small gigs . . ."

And in August, 1967, the Monterey International Pop Festival. The group didn't even have their record released. Mainstream was sitting on it. Janis and Jimi Hendrix got rave reviews and incredible audience reaction, and suddenly, the album was on the streets. It was terrible but, bad as it was, it helped spread the band's name. More important, Clive Davis, president of Columbia Records Division, had been in the audience and liked what he saw and heard. And Albert Grossman, who was in the process of assembling the biggest stable of rock acts in America, was interested.

Monterey was the big break for Big Brother. They had been scheduled to play only on the afternoon show, but the reaction to Janis was so strong that the band was put on the evening show again. The audience was ecstatic once again. It was the beginning of the big time.

Big Brother signed with Albert Grossman in January, 1968. Peter Albin said: "We felt it was important to have someone who was involved in management on a national level working for us. There are a lot more offers and deals being done in L.A. and New York than in San Francisco. We wanted to get out of San Francisco and start touring."

Bill Graham, remembering the old Janis with her original band, said: "I was, as everyone else was, very impressed with this wild, raucous sound coming from Janis . . . the most endearing old story I can remember about Janis is three years ago when I told her I had Otis Redding booked

and she went crazy. And Otis was there for three nights at the old Fillmore and all the local groups wanted to play with him and we had a different group each night. But the thing about Janis was that each night she asked me ahead of time, she said 'Bill, please, please can I come there early before anybody else so I can make sure I see him,' because she idolized Otis. And every night she would come to the ballroom at six o'clock and sit herself down on the main floor, right in the middle, right in front of the stage. She was there before we even opened the building. When we opened there she was with all the other kids and she was leaning against the stage and looking up just like all the other little fans and she was just amazed at his ability, and then she went backstage and was like a baseball fan asking Willie Mays for his autograph . . . I remember that more than any other event in all the times we were privileged to . . . I remember that more than anything.

"I don't think Janis tried to be black. I think Janis sang as a young person coming out of Texas and having kicked around San Francisco, and her voice was her voice and that was her interpretation of the songs. She sang blues. And in her own way . . . you know, when someone is a stylist or the originator of a style and . . . a particular style of blues, I don't think you can compare her. And I keep coming back to Hendrix. Hendrix was an innovator on the guitar, Janis was an innovator in a certain style . . . very few tried to play like Hendrix—you couldn't. Well, Janis was that. The mark of great talent, creative talent and original talent is also in its difficulty to copy that talent. And I think that's what Janis has.

"I recall a time here at the Fillmore in San Francisco, oh, was it a year ago the last time she was here? And she had a death of a cold, and she had some alcoholic beverage with her and some tea on the stage, she grabbed ahold of me and said, 'Bill, I'm so worried. I hope they like me, I'm in my own home town, you think it'll be all right?' The truth is that Janis is one of those people, she couldn't do any wrong here. But even knowing that she was worried and that's what made her what she was. I don't want to knock somebody else, but I figure it's public knowledge that there are a lot of peo-

ple in this industry who say 'I don't give a shit, I'll go out there and do my thing or do the best I can—we'll do 10 numbers or whatever, make some revolutionary statements and tell everybody to get up and dance,' but Janis, you know, they talk about troupers being ready to get up on the stage anytime . . .

"The last time she played New York I called Lindall, who is her roommate here in Larkspur, and I said what is Janis into these days? And she said, 'Well, she likes maroon now—she's buying maroon colors, clothing, whatever —and she's really into guacamole and she's into gin'—this is about a year ago and she's off Comfort. And I called New York. It didn't take much. We painted one of the dressing rooms maroon, put up some nice posters, got a bunch of guacamole and just as an extra touch rented a portable bar and took one of the ushers, who is like one of her real fans, and put him in a tuxedo with a top hat with his long hair and his beard and he schlepped over in a taxi, and she came to rehearsal in the afternoon, and we had just the big tulip in a vase in the dressing room and when she walked in she met Mike, the valet, with the tulip, with the guacamole, with the gin, with the room painted maroon, and it destroyed her —she cried."

By April, 1968, Janis and the band (people had begun to think of it in that way by then) were in New York to record *Cheap Thrills* for Columbia. The band had played the Anderson Theater on Second Avenue the previous February, across from what was known then as the Village Theatre— but with the coming of the San Francisco Sound to New York, would change to the Fillmore *East*. Kip Cohen, who worked for Bill Graham then, as now, said: "There was no question that she was a great star then, as much as she was now. Big Brother was a funky and not-so-good band but everyone loved them because it was Janis and pure San Francisco and the height of the whole thing." (Actually, the Summer of Love had been the *past* season, Hippie had been declared dead, and the Haight had begun to decay. *Musically*, however, it may have been the high point.)

Big Brother had some trouble in the studio. Janis reported that New York had made everyone aggressive. "San

Francisco's different," she told writer Nat Hentoff in the New York Times. "I don't mean it's perfect, but the rock bands there didn't start because they wanted to make it. They dug getting stoned and playing for people dancing . . . What we have to do is learn to control success."

Cheap Thrills, complete with all the Joplin heavies—"Ball and Chain," "Piece of My Heart," etc., came out in September of 1968 and sold a million dollars in copies. Janis was the biggest thing in American rock and roll. Cashbox called her "a mixture of Leadbelly, a steam engine, Calamity Jane, Bessie Smith, an oil derrick and rotgut bourbon funneled into the 20th century somewhere between El Paso and San Francisco." Hentoff said she "was the first white blues singer (female) since Teddy Grace who sang the blues out of black influences but had developed her own sound and phrasing." Bill Graham, asked to talk about her talent as a blues/rock singer recently: "I think Janis was a great performer, one of the few great entertainers in rock . . . as far as being a white blues singer, she moved . . . what else can a man say—you can't say she was better than—she moved me." Janis herself said: "There's no patent on soul. You know how that whole myth of black soul came up? Because white people don't allow themselves to feel things. Housewives in Nebraska have pain and joy; they've got soul if they give in to it. It's hard. And it isn't all a ball when you do."

By November, the rumors of the Holding Company breaking up couldn't be ignored. Janis played her last gig with the band December 1st at the Family Dog for Chet Helms. She'd already begun rehearsing her new band, known variously as The Janis Revue and Main Squeeze, and there were the usual ugly stories making the rounds. Two days after Janis died, Peter Albin recalled what it was like: "It was in New York that she made the decision to split. There were several gigs where all of us would feel down. She'd have done her part with an amount of self assurance, but there was a whole time when the waves started separating. The kind of performance she would put out would be a different trip than the band's. I'd say it was a star trip, where she related to the audience like she was the only one on the stage, and not relating to us at all."

(Albin had been union representative and spokesman for Big Brother, and both he and Janis worked on the production of *Cheap Thrills*—to the chagrin of producer John Simon.)

Sam Andrew, who went on with Janis to her second band, said she fought the split for a long time: "People were telling her that [she was better than the band] very early, but it didn't make any difference . . . then it got pretty intense for six months. Albert was coming on heavy to her. One night at Winterland—I don't know, a couple of guys were sick or something, but afterward she said, 'Man, I go out there and try, and those guys aren't trying.' It was this one night; it was when I noticed the change. And that was the year of soul, too—the year that everyone was into horns and shit—it wasn't hard *feelings*. It was pretty natural. We all saw it coming for quite a while.

From the very beginning the Squeeze had difficulty. The line-up was Sam Andrew, guitar; Bill King, organ; Marcus Doubleday, trumpet; Tony Clemens, tenor (followed by Snooky Flowers); Brad Campbell, bass; and Roy Markowitz, drums; Grossman sent Mike Bloomfield to San Francisco on December 18th, 1968, to try to get the band together, Janis was scheduled to debut in Memphis, Tennessee, three days later at the Memphis Mid-South Coliseum. The occasion was the annual Memphis Sound party, presided over by Stax Records president Jim Stewart. The scheduled acts included the Bar-Kays, Otis Redding's old band, Albert King, the Mad Lads, Judy Clay, Carla and Rufus Thomas, Eddie Floyd and Janis. These were all hard-core Memphis soul acts (excluding King), given to flash and show biz. Janis' band seemed out of place, tuning their instruments and setting up interminably. Half of the crowd had no idea who she was, and the others, white teen-agers, had never heard her do anything but "Ball and Chain" and "Piece of My Heart."

Janis opened with "Raise Your Hand" and followed with the Bee Gees' "To Love Somebody."

There was almost no applause. No encore. Backstage, everyone from her band was in shock. She was told repeatedly that she had sung well, and that the rest had been beyond her control, but she didn't want comfort.

After Memphis, members Marcus Doubleday and Bill King left, and were replaced by Terry Hensley and Richard Kermode. The band did a "sound test" in Rindge, New Hampshire (the most obscure gig the Grossman office could arrange), and then ran a "preview" in Boston before playing the Fillmore East on February 11th and 12th, 1969. It was the biggest event in Eastern rock at that point in the year, and the media was waiting, along with legions of fans.

The first song got only fair response, but things improved when Janis did the Chantells' old hit "Maybe" and "Summertime" from the *Cheap Thrills* album. Janis' hair was flying like a dervish and her long fingers were showing white, clenching a hand mike. "To Love Somebody" was overdone, and so was a new song, "Jazz for the Jack-Offs." The distance between singer and band had never been more apparent. She closed fairly strongly, however, with a then-new Nick Gravenites song, "Work Me Lord."

Later, during an interview, Janis kept interrupting the questions with her own interjections: "Hey, I've never sung so great! Don't you think I'm singing better? Well, Jesus, fucking Christ. I'm really better, believe me."

Reporter Paul Nelson observed: "One gets the alarming feeling that Joplin's whole world is precariously balanced on what happens to her musically—that the necessary degree of honest cynicism needed to survive an all-media assault may be buried too far under the immensely likeable but tremendously underconfident naivete."

By the middle of March, 1969, things had not improved much, and word was that Grossman was asking astronomical amounts for a Joplin appearance. In his column of March 24th, in the San Francisco Chronicle, Ralph J. Gleason wrote: "It was almost impossible to believe it but the fact was that in her first appearance here with her own group, after all the national publicity and all the tremendous sales of her album with Big Brother and the Holding Company, her opening night audience at Winterland did not bring her back for an encore.

"Her new band is a drag. They can play OK but they are a pale version of the Memphis-Detroit bands from the rhythm & blues shows and Janis, though in good voice, seems bent on becoming Aretha Franklin. The best things they did were the things which were most like her songs with Big Brother . . .

"The best things that could be done would be for her to scrap this band and go right back to being a member of Big Brother . . . (if they'll have her)."

In the April 19 issue of *Rolling Stone*, Random Notes reported: "The whole Janis Joplin hype has grown to outrageous proportions, whereby impossible goals have been established for her. No singer could deliver an absolute organ with every phrase—not Billie Holiday, not Edith Piaf, not Aretha—and yet somehow Janis is supposed to."

In May, 1969, the British pop newspaper Melody Maker carried an interview with Joplin. The following is an excerpt:

"Janis was to have been on the cover of Newsweek . . . but General Eisenhower's death had elbowed her out. [She was shown the discarded Newsweek cover photo and] in quick succession came a display of pleasure at the way the photo came out and anger at the fact it wouldn't be seen. She grasped it in her hands, stared at it for an instant, stamped her tiny foot bullet-like into the . . . floor and swung a clenched fist skyward. A stream of devastating curses accompanied the action. 'God-dammit, you mother—#&!3! You *%#"!' And swinging round to appeal to the gathering: "Fourteen heart attacks and he had to die in my week. In MY week."

In August, Janis turned in a great performance at the Atlantic City Pop Festival in New Jersey, and in September her attorney considered bringing suit against a television actress for an ad hype. In November her *Kozmic Blues* album was released to generally favorable reviews. The vocal excesses seemed to have been under control, and the material "Maybe," "Try," "Little Girl Blue," "Kozmic Blues" and "As Good As You've Been to This World" was considered "better."

The Revue played its last gig in Madison Square Garden on December 29th, and the next day, Janis announced she'd "gotten together" with Joe Namath, and dedicated her concert

to him. Following the concert Clive Davis threw an elegant party for her at his Central Park West apartment and Bob Dylan, one of her old idols, showed up.

On March 4, 1970, she was fined $200 (in absentia) in a court in Tampa, Florida after having been found guilty of using profane language during a concert the previous year. Janish had reportedly screamed at police who were trying to keep teenagers from dancing.

On March 20 she announced from a hotel in Rio de Janeiro that "I'm going into the jungle with a big bear of a beatnik named David Niehaus. I finally remembered I don't have to be on stage 12 months a year. I've decided to go and dig some other jungles for a couple of weeks." Janis met Niehaus in Rio, where she'd gone as part of a three-month vacation. When she returned, she got two tattoos, one on her wrist, and one over her heart. "A little something for the boys," she said.

In mid-April Janis appeared with Big Brother and the Holding Company's reformed band (Nick Gravenites had been added to the old members; Sam Andrew was also back with them), at the Fillmore West. She did all of her old numbers, even "Easy Rider" from the Mainstream album and "Cuckoo" from *Cheap Thrills*. "We're really dredgin' up the past for ya, folks," Janis chuckled.

The band was much better technically than they'd ever been, but, as in the old days, it was Janis that the crowd wanted. She reportedly allowed a blind person to touch her.

On June 12 she and her new band, Full-Tilt Boogie, debuted at Freedom Hall in Louisville, Kentucky. There were only 4,000 persons in attendance in the monster indoor stadium, but the show was a knock-out. As soon as Janis began her jiving introduction to "Try" —"Honey if you've had your eye on a piece of talent and that chick down the road has been getting all the action, then you know what you gotta do . . . *Try*, just a little bit harder!"—the crowd began dancing and screaming. "I permit them to dance," she told a burly guard who tried to repress some of the audience.

The Boogie band's members include John Till, lead guitar and Brad Campbell, bass, both of whom were with her

in the Revue. The new members are Richard Bell, piano, a former Ronnie Hawkins sideman, and Clark Pierson, a drummer Janis found in a North Beach topless bar.

Everyone who saw them agreed that Janis had finally assembled a band that could back her, who could provide the push she felt she needed.

Her last appearance with them was at Harvard Stadium on August 12th, before 40,000 people. Both Janis and the band then went into recording sessions in Los Angeles. Her album with the new group had been tentatively scheduled for a November or December release date.

Janis Joplin's last public appearance anywhere was in September. She showed up in Port Arthur, Texas for the 10th annual reunion of her graduating class of 1960, Thomas Jefferson High School. She wore flowing blue and pink feathers in her hair, purple and white satin and velvet with gold embroidery, sandals and painted toenails, and rings and bracelets enough for a Babylonian whore.

Janis and entourage swept into the Goodhue Hotel's drab Petroleum Room and commandeered the bar. When she asked for vodka (she'd switched to gin and vodka from Southern Comfort about a year ago), the bartender said he had nothing but bourbon and scotch. "God," she said. "Somebody go out and get a bottle of vodka."

Port Arthur has never seen the like of her.

Last December Janis had finally escaped her adopted city, where she'd lived in the Haight-Ashbury across from Buena Vista Park and Hippie Hill and, later, on Noe Street near the southern tip of downtown San Francisco. She found a hideaway home in Larkspur, across the Golden Gate Bridge, three or four towns into Marin County.

Larkspur is one of those pleasant little places. The freeway leads comfortably into a small shopping center; the homes are respectable, middle class. Then, somewhere, you make a left turn and several roads take you into the woods. Baltimore Avenue is one of those roads, its width narrowed by huge trees that block its way now and again. Janis' house was at the end of Baltimore.

It's hidden away more by its appearance than by its location. It's right there in front of you, behind the rounded off end of the road. Short, A-framed, shingled, modern, comfortable in a forest of tall trees that keep everything but the wind away. You can't even hear the sound of kids at Larkspur School, just up the road and a few blocks over.

The house is unidentified. A Yuban coffee can is nailed to a front post. "This is a temporary mail box," it is labeled, and someone has added, "Temporary Hell." Near the adjacent garage, two dogs are wandering around. A TV cameraman waves his light meter at the air, then pans his camera from the wooden stairs near the garage that lead into the woods. He pans across the house, to the fence Janis had had constructed to keep burglars away.

This wasn't a very private or a very quiet house for Janis and the girl friends who stayed there. The place was burglarized several times, and Janis and her clothesmaker/friend, Lindall Erb, lost furnishings, jewelry, and other valuables. Several months ago, Janis had a party there that resulted in complaints from the neighbors. Cars clogged the road all the way up Baltimore Avenue, and the music blared out of that shingled megaphone as far as the cars went.

Now the TV cameraman is back in his car—one of three cars parked facing the house. A high school girl is seated 100 feet away, watching. "I came here from Mill Valley to pay my tribute," she said. "I'm just an acquaintance. I came by once and gave her a bottle of tequila and it got her off . . ."

Up the road, two neighbors, grandmotherly women, are talking. They're saying something about "overdose" to a couple of kids on bicycles. One of the women talks with a smirk. "Oh, did she have parents? . . . There was a lot of noise when the band was practicing —if you call it a band . . . We never talked to her. She just ran down and ran up again in her car."

"I don't think we'll make the 7 o'clock news," the other, named Betsy, says with a laugh.

Inside the house, it's quiet. One man, a member of Janis' second band—the one after Big Brother—steps out to get something from his car. Lindall is in L.A., he says. She left the night before, when she heard the news. The people in the home are friends of Lindall's. And no one wants to talk.

The two old ladies have stopped looking at the TV man, and they're discussing reupholstering an old couch sitting in Betsy's front yard.

—*October 29, 1970*

JOHN COOKE TELLS HOW IT WAS

The following was written by John Cooke, a long-time friend of Janis Joplin and road manager for the Full Tilt Boogie Band, her last group. Cooke discovered Janis' body in the Landmark Motor Hotel on Sunday, October 4th, and so is in the best position to clarify details that seemed confusing at the time of her death. Rolling Stone's account of how Janis was found was based on interviews with Paul Rothschild, the producer of her last album, and Robert Gordon, her attorney. Cooke was unavailable for comment at presstime, although our reporters tried repeatedly to reach him.

BY JOHN COOKE

JANIS IS GONE and nothing can change that. It seems trivial to be concerned with details surrounding the event, but the lead article in the October 29th ROLLING STONE gives Janis' death an aura of melodrama that simply was not present. She died by accident at just the time when everything in her life was coming together. Nick Gravenites said it well.

Early in the evening of October 4th I got a call from Seth Morgan [Janis' fiance]. He was at the San Francisco airport, I was at the Landmark Hotel in Hollywood. He was looking for Janis, who was going to meet him at the Burbank airport. He had called the studio where Paul Rothschild and the Full Tilt Boogie were working on the record and found her not there. I asked if Paul was expecting her at a particular time and he said he hadn't asked. I told Seth I was on my way to the studio and would talk to Paul and locate Janis before he arrived in Burbank, and for him to call the studio when he got in.

I was leaving the hotel with Vince Mitchell and Phil Badella, Janis' equipment men, when we saw her car in the driveway. We'd been meaning to get down to the studio earlier and were in a hurry now, but I thought Janis might have just got back to the hotel and I decided to check her room. I went straight to the desk and got a key; then I went in and found Janis.

I re-locked the room and went back to the garage where I told Vince and Phil and another friend of mine who was with us. We phoned Bob Gordon, Janis' lawyer, first, then Albert Grossman in Bearsville. Bob Gordon called his brother-in-law, a doctor who arrived at the hotel shortly after Bob.

Bob Gordon and I notified the hotel manager, Jack Hagy. (A wonderful man who loved Janis and did innumerable things that evening and in the days that followed to help us in many touching ways.) He and Bob Gordon called the police and I called Janis' parents. Before the police and coroner's office arrived (discreetly), I went to the studio to tell Paul Rothschild and the band. It had been 7:30 when I found Janis. It was now about 9:00 PM and from that point the news spread rapidly. We tried to call many people close to Janis, to reach them before they heard the news on the radio.

Two things which were also reported erroneously in the R.S. article should be made clear: no one except men from the coroner's office moved the body, and no one except the police department and the coroner's office searched Janis' room.

Also, the $4.50 found in Janis' hands was explained a few days later when the night clerk remembered that Janis had come out to the desk shortly after arriving at the hotel from Barney's Beanery about 1:00 AM Sunday morning. She had a $5 bill and needed change for cigarettes. The full pack of cigarettes was found near her.

The interview with Nick Gravenites gives a good picture of the days before Janis' death. She was very happy. She had a man she loved, and she was more pleased with her music than I had ever seen her before. The last breakthrough on the new record had happened and the end was in sight. She was looking forward to being taken away for a vacation with her man and then doing a great fall tour. On Saturday night she left the studio with a couple of the boys and went to Barney's. She had been drinking Ripple at the studio and had two drinks, of vodka if you can believe that, at Barney's. She drove back to the hotel with Ken Pearson, her organ player, and went to her room. Except for when she came out to get cigarettes a few minutes later, that was the last anyone saw of her. There is not the slightest trace of suspicion in my mind that her death might have been intentional. She didn't believe in cutting short a rocking good time, and that's what she was having.

Other points that should be made clear are:

1. It is true that Janis had signed a will a few days before her death, but the R.S. article failed to mention that this was not her first will. She had recently made a few changes not related to any recent events, and had simply signed the new will.

2. The R.S. article mentioned an unidentified "source" at Columbia who said the record had "not been going well." That's bullshit. We have since checked with the only three people at Columbia Records who knew anything at all about Janis' sessions and none of them was the "source" for that statement. No one else was competent to comment because no one else knew anything about the progress of the recordings. The statement is either a reporter's invention or else some cretin at Columbia was on a weird ego trip.

3. The article went into a good deal of past history about Janis' various bands and a few musicians were left out. No one who played in those bands should be left out because at some time or other every band Janis sang with made great music. The Kozmic Blues band, as we're now in the habit of calling it, was very underrated although their magic, like Big Brother's, was never adequately captured on records. And they did have magic, of a very different kind. When they were really on everyone loved it, including Janis, but among the various personalities and musical directions in the band there were never enough elements that meshed together enough of the time for the group to become the perfect backup band for Janis. But they really had their moments and there are some music fans around who remember, and somewhere maybe even a critic or two.

The only two musicians who were with the Kozmic Blues band throughout the year of existence are Brad Campbell (bass) and Terry Clements (alto sax). Bill King was the original organ player but the Army started chasing him after two gigs and he was replaced by Richard Kermode who stayed for the duration. Roy Markowitz was the drummer for about half of the year, followed for a week (during some of the recording sessions) by Lonnie Castille and then by Maury Baker. After Sam Andrew left, John Till brought his guitar to the group and has been with Janis ever since. Marcus Doubleday played trumpet briefly and decided the road was not for him anymore. He was followed first by Terry Hensley and then by Luis Gasca, who was with the band for more than eight months. (More than a few people were first astonished and then entranced to hear a trace of *mariachi* playing around an octave or so above Janis' voice while Luis was with the band. It turned me on almost every time.) In the last few weeks Luis was followed by Dave Woodward. Snooky Flowers (tenor sax) was added to the band early along, and was in it to the end. They're a good bunch.

Janis was blissfully happy with the Full Tilt Boogie. From the start everything meshed and kept on meshing, getting tighter and tighter. They are great musicians: Ken Pearson (organ), Brad Campbell (bass), John Till (guitar), Richard Bell (piano, the real kind), and Clark Pierson (drums). It looks like they are going to stay together; long may they play. I don't know how everyone at *Rolling Stone* missed it, but they played their first gig at the Hell's Angels' dance last May.

4. Paul Rothschild does not work for Elektra. He has been an independent producer for more than a year. He was not "hired" in the traditional sense to do this album. He and Janis both thought it would be a good idea after one day last July when Janis, Paul, Lindall and I got thoroughly wrecked on *pina colada* at Janis' house. When we ran out of rum we retired to the No Name bar for the evening. It was a good day. The next morning Paul said to me, "John, I found out something wonderful yesterday." "What's that?" I asked. "Janis Joplin is a *very* smart woman," he said. Janis and Paul worked well together. When we had been in the studio for about six weeks Paul would be explaining to her how he was going to accomplish some production miracle and she would be taking words right out of his mouth. He said she was the only woman he ever met who had the head to be a record producer and Janis was really proud of that.

Women's Lib is going to get their backs up over that "only woman" thing, but fuck 'em. We're the last of the unashamed male chauvinists and Janis loved it. She said "I'm for equal pay and all that shit, but hell, man, I don't want to light my own cigarettes and open doors for myself, you know what I mean?"

It's been lonely here in Hollywood for the last two weeks, but Janis is still here in the music. Part of her will be in every note the Full Tilt Boogie ever plays. The record is great and we love it. She was proud of it. We hope you love it as much as she did.

From Janis to you: Keep On Rockin'!

—*November 12, 1970*

AN INTERVIEW WITH JANIS'S FATHER

BY CHET FLIPPO

PORT ARTHUR, Tex.—It is difficult to imagine Janis Joplin in such surroundings. Port Arthur is just a little oil refinery town of maybe 70,000 persons, tucked away in the southeast corner of Texas, a bastion of Middle America. Her death went unnoticed or ignored by most of the populace, who knew only that she was some kind of hippie singer who was ungrateful to her Port Arthur heritage and who had occasionally maligned their town.

Because of this, the sentiment after her death was not totally unexpected. "My God! I hope they don't bring her back here for the funeral. We'll be overrun with hippies," was the stock man-in-the-street reaction recorded in the local paper.

The Joplin home is a neat, tree-shaded pink frame house in a comfortable neighborhood. It is a long way from the Fillmore.

Janis' father, Seth Joplin, the supervisor of one of Texaco's three Port Arthur plants, is sitting in the Joplin living room. It is spotless and orderly, down to the copies of Bazaar and Nation's Business displayed on the coffee table, but is almost choked with flowers sent by well-wishers. At Seth Joplin's right is an enormous stack of telegrams, cards, and letters from all over the world. One card says, "I know what happened. Janis killed herself out of sorrow over Jimi Hendrix's death." That draws wry chuckles from Seth and the interviewer.

Seth, a quiet, introspective man, has agreed today to talk for the family. His wife, Dorothy, is resting. Their son, Mike is at work and daughter Laura is away at college. He settles himself on the couch and lights the first of many cigarettes.

Do you feel the media have been fair to Janis, both before and since her death?

No. By and large the media have not been fair, although they have been fairer since her death. I guess it's harder to attack someone in death. Even so—much of what has been printed has been totally untrue. Since her death there has been so much speculation—and that's all it is. The coroner's report won't be issued for two weeks yet. The newspapers said it was an overdose. They don't know that it was. We were out there in Los Angeles and there were no drugs found in the room. There were some sleeping pills. There might have been an accidental overdose of those. No one knows yet.

Most news reports seemed to dwell on the fact that she had "run away from home." My impression was that she simply went away to college and didn't come back much after that.

She didn't run away from home. There was never any violent separation. I've seen stories that said she ran away from home when she was 11, or 14, or 17. She left home with our approval and our funds. It was not approval in the strictest sense. We would have preferred that she didn't do it, but there wasn't much that we could do about it . . . but the media have been quick to seize upon superficialities without knowing what she was like. She was trusting and lonely and put on all the hell-raising to cover up. Yes, she was a wild woman and a willful child. She cursed and carried on. That was her act, but it was mostly act. Although she led a wild life and tried everything there was to try.

But that isn't the full story . . .

No. Now the papers are trying to sensationalize her. In the past, for ex-

ample, there have been interviews printed that never took place, written by people who never met her. She didn't try to show her best side. She showed what she thought was her individual self. Since her death, I haven't watched many of the TV reports but I've read some of the news reports and they're more sympathetic now.

How did the family hear of her death?

We heard about the death about one AM Monday. John Cooke [her road manager and friend] called us after he discovered her in the motel room. They had recorded Saturday night and then she went back to her room. I heard she was in excellent spirits and happy over the record. Then she wasn't seen all day Sunday, which wasn't like her.

Would you have preferred that she be buried here?

The disposition was handled the way she wanted it. Cremation. And what she wanted was what we wanted.

What was she like as a child?

She went to church, sang in the choir and glee club, and painted. She was an artist, a good one. But she quit because she didn't think she would be as good as she wanted. She was a real nice, bright, smart child.

When was she born?

January 19, 1943, in Port Arthur. She finished high school right after her 17th birthday. She was really a little young for her contemporaries. She was advanced a grade, so she was at least a year younger than everyone else in her class, which we felt was one of her problems. She was emotionally not as mature as she was mentally at that time. From about the age of 14, Janis was a revolutionary—dressing and acting differently.

When did she start college?

The summer after she graduated from high school, she started at Lamar Tech [Lamar Tech College of Technology in nearby Beaumont]. She was studying art, I think. She went to Lamar Tech three different times and the University of Texas two different times. And she went to Port Arthur College where she learned keypunch and then went out to the West Coast and worked in Los Angeles and San Francisco. Before, in Port Arthur, she worked in the library here one summer, was a waitress for awhile, and addressed envelopes. She really got on the beatnik scene, or whatever you want to

call it, her senior year in high school.

Was she pretty much a loner in high school?

Yes, she mostly kept to herself. She had a pretty rough time of it in high school. She insisted on dressing and acting differently and they hated her for it. There were no people she could relate with, talk to. As far as Port Arthur was concerned, she was one of the first revolutionary youth. There's lots of them now.

Was she doing much singing before she left?

No, I don't think she paid much attention to singing. She said once that she was at a party one night and tried imitating Bessie Smith, and I guess that's the way it was. She was doing a lot of painting then, going to parties, reading. She was gone a lot, running around.

Do you recall what type of music she listened to?

No. I don't recall her listening to music much. We had Bach and Beethoven going and she liked some of that. I don't remember what she listened to, other than Bessie Smith and Leadbelly and some of those old blues singers. She listened to them. Her records, most of them, are still around here. I remember when she came back from Austin, she had a guitar and was playing and singing. And at Lamar Tech the last time, she sang at coffeehouses and sang at some in Houston and Austin and around. Mostly, she sang for drinks, but I think she made some money in Austin. At Lamar Tech, she was doing real well, making straight As, but at the end of the term, she lost them. She came back here for summer school, but met up with Big Brother's manager and the next I heard, she was in California and been there ever since.

Something else that has been made much of in articles was alienation from her family. Was that so?

She was never alienated from the family. Although we disagreed with the way she lived, she liked us and we liked her. She came back more than I would have thought.

Did she noticeably change?

No, she remained the same person basically. Although the one-night stands ruined her health, never eating right, living in motels and going to parties. She was driving herself too hard. She never thought about the day after tomorrow. She abused herself physically, there's no doubt about that.

The last time she was here, for the Jefferson High school reunion in August, did she still seem about the same to you?

At the reunion, she seemed very much the same. I never did understand why she came back for it, it was so out of character for her. Maybe the ten years made her a little nostalgic. She was just the same. She never seemed to sleep, always in motion, people always around her. It was never dull around her, even when she was a kid.

Did Janis ever have many friends in Port Arthur?

No, she never had many local friends. People were kind of afraid of her, they didn't know what she might do. Apparently since her death more people here were her friends than she knew. We didn't have any idea of all the friends she had everywhere. We've gotten flowers and messages from all over the world. Something strange, we got as many cards from North Carolina as from Port Arthur. Just like with anybody else—while you're alive people remember the bad things. When you're dead, they remember the good things. She said so much bad about Port Arthur, the people and the media here didn't like her. You'd be surprised at the number of obscene phone calls. While she was alive, we'd get them mostly after she was on TV. Since her death, they've mostly been persons laughing or just silent callers.

We got one call from a girl in Lake Charles, Louisiana. She had run away to Los Angeles to be an actress and she was working as a waitress there when she met Janis in a restaurant, she waited on her. They got to talking and Janis told her to get back home. Janis took her to the bus station, bought her a ticket, and put her on a bus for Lake Charles. She called us up to say how much she appreciated that. She's now married and has a child and she said she would have gone wrong if she had stayed in L.A.

That's not the sort of thing that was usually associated with Janis.

No. That's a side of Janis no one saw. She would only do that if no one was around that she knew, if none of her friends were around. She didn't want to reveal her true feelings.

Were you at all surprised by her success?

No, I wasn't really surprised at her success. Like with her art, she generally managed to do well at whatever she tried. But when she would start to be really good at something, she would quit. I really expected her to quit music.

Did she talk to you much about her music, her success?

She liked the adulation of the crowd. It was her whole life. But you'd be surprised at how lonely a person like that could be—one night stands and motels. She had no stable life of any kind. About a year ago, she bought a house north of San Francisco and was fixing it up at the time of her death. It was a nice place, back in the redwoods. She really liked it, she was very happy about the house and her dogs.

Did she ever express any unhappiness?

She wasn't dissatisfied with life. She remarked about the loneliness of it, the lack of stability, the lack of friends. But that's just the way her life was.

What sort of paintings did she do?

She painted practically everything, even some religious themes, although she was never a religious person. One night she had a painting she wanted to do, on a great big canvas, six or eight feet long. So she took it out into the garage. It was a cold winter night and she ran the clothes dryer for heat and painted out there all night long.

What was the subject?

It was of the Three Kings. But she painted it as her feeling of the Three Kings. One painting that we still have, which is unfinished, is of Christ on the cross, very cubistic. My wife plans to finish it herself. She was a singer in high school and got a voice scholarship to Texas Christian University. But she quit singing after college.

Had you heard much about the progress of the new album?

They had eight songs finished out of the ten that were planned for the album. I think it will be released in the middle of November. Of course they want to capitalize on it. While I was in L.A. one of the papers there had a kind of James Dean thing about Janis, saying she died before she reached her prime. Her managers thought she was just coming into her best singing. That's what Albert Grossman said. She had a band this time that she really liked, that suited her style. They were

willing to play as a back-up group, rather than as individuals. Big Brother wasn't really good enough, they didn't care. The brass in her second group didn't suit her. Her voice was like an orchestra in itself. But this new group was just right for her. This will be far and away her best record. I didn't particularly like the others.

Did you ever see her perform?

We saw her shortly after the Monterey Pop Festival. We saw her at the Fillmore and I'll never get over that. I couldn't imagine the volume of sound —truly incredible. But she was good. The band put on a special performance free for our benefit. And we saw her twice in Houston, at the Coliseum and the Music Hall.

Are Janis' brother or sister musically inclined?

Laura [who is 21 and a graduate student in psychology at Southern Methodist University in Dallas] plays guitar and has a sweet little voice, as far as folk songs go, songs like "Long Black Veil." I think she's really good at it. She was youth director at her church here and she sang there. She graduated from Lamar Tech in three years.

What about Mike?

Michael is 17 and he's kind of a willful one, too. It ain't easy. But he's a real nice boy. He could be an artist, he's good at drawing. He can look at something small and draw it larger in perfect proportion. Janis could do the same, but she blocked things. He doesn't have to.

*   *   *

We both fell silent and a strange, tangible, almost uncomfortable stillness fills the room. Seth stands, signaling the end of the talk, and says, "She was a pretty good kid, really, in most ways. As a parent you look at her differently. She wasn't easy to raise, but then a lot of people aren't. Maybe you weren't."

On the way out, Seth took me to the garage to show me something he had found while cleaning it out earlier in the day. He points to the floor, saying, "See those? She scratched those into the concrete when she was just a kid."

There, in two corners of the garage, are "JANIS" and "JLJ" (Janis Lyn Joplin).

—November 12, 1970

THE SADDEST STORY IN THE WORLD

Nick Gravenites met Janis Joplin almost ten years ago in San Francisco. When she left Big Brother, it was Mike Bloomfield and Gravenites that she turned to, and Nick composer/vocalist with Electric Flag, gave her both counsel and compositions. She was set to record a new Gravenites tune, to wrap up her Full-Tilt Boogie album, when she died. Gravenites now gigs with the recently reorganized Big Brother and the Holding Company band and is producing their album, on which Janis makes a "cameo appearance," as he puts it.

Ben Fong-Torres spoke to Nick two days after Janis died.

Where'd you meet Janis?

I met her at the Coffee Gallery in North Beach, way before she joined Big Brother. She was playing autoharp and singing country stuff at the time— country blues, country music in general. It was that time where David Crosby was playing there; Dino Valenti. I hit town about 1959 and I guess this is about '61 or '62.

Then she went back to Texas and came back out when Chet called her a few years later. How did you meet her again when she'd joined Big Brother?

I was in Chicago at the time, running a club called the Burning Bush, a blues club. And Big Brother came to play at Mother Blues. This is when they came to Chicago and signed the Mainstream contract, the one they regretted. It seems like that whole Chicago trip was very important to them. They didn't realize what heavy drinking was until they hit Chicago, and they didn't really know what the blues were. By the time they left, they realized what it was all about.

First of all they got fucked . . . I don't think they got paid all the money they were supposed to get paid at the gig and then they met a lot of hard-drinking people and then they realized the only thing they could do in Chicago to stay alive was drink a lot. Then they got hit on to sign the Mainstream contract and they got a supposedly good Chicago lawyer, and it turned out the lawyer also represented the record company. Totally fucked them bad. They were playing at Mother Blues,

and all the local hippie, hipster types would show up and dig them. But they were so freaky at the time, all of them had long hair, Janis looked so weird with her long granny gown and her shrieking voice, and people didn't know what the fuck to make of them. At the time I was talking to this record producer, who produced suburban Chicago music, like the Shadows of Knight, you know, the high school stuff, and he was shaking his head and saying, "Gee, they're nice; it's too bad no one will pick them up." Even to him it was obvious they were just too too outrageous for any sane thinking person to even consider recording or getting involved with at that level. And maybe one daring adventurous person would get up to dance. It was just one of those scenes, where they were like on Mars.

Did they seek out the contract that led them to Mainstream, or did Mainstream for some reason go to them and ask them to sign?

I think it was Mainstream that hit on them. It was probably the only label that hit on them. When I found out about the deal I was incredulous, you know. They got maybe $100—they still haven't got any money out of those people. When they signed with Columbia, Columbia had to pay Mainstream $250,000, which, the band had to pay back to Columbia, you dig. It fucked them bad, sold a lot of records, never paid them anything on it, and then accepted a quarter-million from Columbia to get off the contract. They had Chet Helms as a manager, and everybody knows Chet is a nice guy but . . .

They came to Chicago as part of the San Francisco scene. One of the first bands that came was the Jefferson Airplane but they were more folk oriented, and people in that club could understand it more. Big Brother were just the freaks.

The audience was dumbfounded. They didn't know whether they should get up and dance; they didn't know whether they should like them or not.

What was your reaction?

I was a little scared, to tell you the truth. I was no different. They scared the hell out of me. Especially Janis. Reeking of patchouly and madras dress on and covered with pimples. She had this weird voice—I think she had a sore throat at the time and it sounded even weirder.

I just didn't know what to do. I had this short haircut, when they saw me on the street. They were on one side of the street and I was on the other. I looked over and I recognized them. So I started to cross the street, but they didn't recognize me, and at the time I was in my Chicago bag, they thought I was some big greasy gangster that was crossing the street to come over and fuck with them, like to beat them up or something. It wasn't until I got two feet from them that they recognized me. They thought they were going to get assaulted, you know, they were getting a lot of weird reactions in town.

But was Janis basically the same person?

Yeah, sure. She was funky, and she was still alone. She was so weird that not too many people could emphathize with her; nobody understood her. It wasn't until later that she started getting into a more sexy dress bag and a more sexy approach. At that time she was covered with sack cloth and screaming the blues.

Did you work with Big Brother at all?

No. I was busy with the Flag. You see, I had known Gurley for years. He and I were folk blues cats on North Beach together years ago. And he was a blues guitarist and I was and we played the same gigs and we were good friends. Then I knew Peter Albin. But they had their thing, and I had mine. We were both pushing it. It didn't get together until Janis left Big Brother and she was trying to get something together for herself. And at that time the Flag had been busted up and she took some of the members of the Flag as part of her band. And Michael Bloomfield and I tried to help her with some of the arrangements and stuff but we couldn't get too far.

Did Janis turn to you and Michael?

Well, she wanted to turn to anyone that she felt was competent that could do it. Michael was so headstrong—like he had his own set way of doing things, and it just conflicted too much with Janis' ego, even though she wanted him to work on her music more.

She really couldn't tell the difference between a good drummer and a bad drummer, between someone who was a decent saxophone player and someone who was just shucking. So essentially that was my and Michael's role—saying, "Don't get crazy, he did all right, he can play drums." Stuff like that. She had a concept before she started. She wanted to have a soul band. She wanted to be at the same level as the really professional blues and soul singers, like Aretha and those people. She wanted to have at least the same kind of band, the same kind of horn men. The more professional approach to music.

And probably the reason she left Big Brother was the reviews that magazines and newspapers would write. Janis Joplin, out of sight, outrageous, this and that. Big Brother: dog shit. And so after reading review after review like this she got real crazy, and she felt she'd have to drop the band and get a band together who were really good as musicians, not necessarily hotshot writers or having their own thing, but just professional musicians, who could really arrange and do stuff like that. Well, it didn't work out quite that way. There was so much tension involved—what to be done, how to do it—expectations. And Janis didn't quite know what the hell was happening, either—she'd never done it before, and there was a whole lot of speculation. It was really kind of a crazy period.

What was your role with the new band?

It was pretty much the same role. Going over there and just making a judgment as to whether they were competent musicians or not. And it was a lot easier this trip because her new band pretty much came as a unit. Well, the holdover she kept from her old band, Brad, her bass player, knew all the new cats that showed up that were all Canadians, from Ronnie Hawkins' band, and they were playing together for a long time. They were glad to be reunited with Brad and they had a very high feeling of camaraderie, and good fellowship—it was an organized band; it wasn't a whole bunch of cats that didn't know each other. I immediately realized that it was that kind of scene.

Janis at the time was really upset. She was saying, "Fifty people help Joe Cocker and Leon Russell helps Joe Cocker and all these people help Joe Cocker and all these people are helping these people and why doesn't anybody help me?" She was upset. So essentially that's what I was doing at that time. I would chase around—I'd go

over to Tom Donahue's, and I would say, Tom, Janis feels let down. "How is it that certain people can command a lot of fellowship and respect and help other people and I can't?" And then Tom would go through every one of his old records that he loved and then he'd go over there and he'd sit around and say, "Janis, here's a tune maybe you'd like on this album, here's something maybe you'd like on that." And she loved 'em, man. She picked up maybe five or six tunes off Donahue.

And then I'd go around and I'd tell people the same story, and people started to show up and turn her on to things. Michael would show up and help her with some arrangement and stuff. People would bring tunes.

She mentioned that there were a couple of songs by you for this next album.

It's the saddest story in the world. She had eight tunes done, five of which had the final vocals, three of which had work vocals. What happened was, I saw her Monday and Tuesday, I went down to L.A., I got a call Thursday night from Paul Rothschild and he said Janis had eight tunes, she wanted to get one or two more—they'd spent the last two or three days in the studio looking at each other and did I have any new material for her. And I told him that I'd written about four or five tunes that week, and I thought one or two of them she might like. Early Monday morning I flew down to Los Angeles and I had some mixing to do at CBS for Big Brother's album and I did a little work there and then I went over to Rothschild's house with Janis—I met Janis at the motel—and tried to play some tapes I had, but the machine was—well, look, I've got this one tune called "Buried Alive in Blues." It's sort of incomplete, I've got a couple of verses on it, let me work on it. So what happened was the next day, I finished up the tune. And I took it to her that evening at the rehearsal, and I taught the band the song and I taught Janis the words and everybody loved the tune, and then I left town. Then Rothschild called me, and said, "Man, the band worked on the tune even more, changed it around, so the arrangement was even more spectacular than the one you taught us, we went into the studio and the band cut the band track for us, and Janis came

that night, and dug the band track and totally freaked out and jumped up and down and her bells were ringing."

She was going to come back the next day and do the vocal, but she died that night. And so that was going to be the last tune on her album; it was incomplete, she never got to sing it. Paul asked me to come down to finish the tune, to sing the tune. I told him I'd do anything he wanted me to do, but it was just one of those things that I was just laughing and crying at the same time—the story was just too incredibly sad. I couldn't even think straight. So that was that—I don't know what the hell to say—it's a sad story.

The band got together and they had a meeting and they all want to go back and finish the album, get it done right. And they want to finish it. Paul Rothschild says he's got another few things on the album too, like a birthday present for John Lennon or something, a tape, and a few other little things that she sang acappella and that sort of thing. That's going to be on the album too.

Do you have any idea whether or not her band will still stay together?

I don't know—it's such a change. They're all such great, sweet cats. They were just riding the crest.

Not to mention Janis—she was just as happy as she's ever been.

Well, I'll tell you, she was so happy when I was talking to her. She was telling me everything about her new old man and how there were wedding bells in the air and they were going to get married and she finally dug an old man that she could relate to—and she was so happy with her band it was sad, because she felt that she had to sing even better to get as good as the band was playing. The band was playing so good she felt she really had to get better than she was just to get up to their level. She was so happy, man, the album was almost done—I mean as happy as anyone could be in L.A.

How long was she in Los Angeles?

A month. And you know L.A. It's the kind of place where if you're stuck in a motel room—you don't know *what* it can drive you to do.

Did you ever know Janis to mess around with hard drugs?

She told me that she used to be, a long time ago, a meth freak. I mean a run-down, crazy-ass meth freak, the kind you see on the street, with the little fine polished crust of dirt around their eyes. But she beat it. She beat it and she told me she never wanted to get into that bag again. But in this whole rock scene there's—it's like a prison, really—that's the way I find it talking to people—there's a lot of people using junk in the rock scene, and they're on death row, the rest of them on Tier C. The ones that abuse themselves the most in terms of hard drugs, or really excessive anything, drinking or whatever, they're automatically put on death row. It's just a way of enduring because you know they're going to die, you know it. So people are just figuring out ways to cushion the blow when it happens.

You get calloused about it, in a way. How can you relate to a good friend of yours that is using junk? What do you do? Nothing works to get them off of it. So you put them in a bag—you say this person is going to die on me. Get ready for it so when it happens you don't get too crazy on it. And that whole blues scene is that way. Even this year all the young blues cats were dying in Chicago, older than Janis, but not much more than 10 or 15 years older—they did it with alcohol, wine, just bad living.

And she lived that kind of life—it was a funky life—she was a down-to-earth chick. She was a star, but she was right down to earth. She didn't have all these hangups about stardom, she didn't feel that everything she had to say was important and people would write it down—and she wasn't stuck up or snobbish. She didn't feel that she had a corner on the hip world like a lot of the rock stars do and she didn't get into any of this exploitation shit where something would happen in the newspapers and a week later she'd have a tune out on it. It's really—the road she took wasn't the pop star role. She had such a fantastic personality that a lot of people picked up on it, TV, papers and stuff and people got freaked out behind it, but basically, she dug her friends and got real funky and never lost it. I can't say the same about a lot of other people.

But she was depressed for a while about being ostracized in San Francisco.

San Francisco is a very funny music scene and I'm still considered an outsider to the scene even though I've been

here 12 or 13 years. It's sort of like a booster club, the Junior Chamber of Commerce where if it's San Francisco it's cool, and that's the only way you should think about it—if you live here that's what's happening. If it's from San Francisco it's swinging. If you think it's not, then you're an asshole, "what are you trying to do, tear down our scene?"

Janis had a more universal view of music—if it was good it was good and it didn't matter if it was San Francisco or if it was Memphis, Texas, Chicago, it didn't make any difference. Good music is good music and this chauvinistic San Francisco scene—well, tough luck. Because it's just turned into who can buy the most cocaine. The fancy clothes and the $10,000 cocaine deals, that's to me where it's gotten.

It sounds like you're talking about just one or two bands.

Yeah, you're right, you're right. I'm talking about just one or two of the more successful ones.

The whole Janis thing is the saddest story. She had her new house, she had all her tasteful furniture that she went out and bought, and she had her pool table, and she had the landscape people come in and put fences in, remodeling this and that, she had her life together, she had her own little corporation, and just everything revolved around her. She loved her new house, she had her life figured out with Grossman—they got together, so that all she had to do was work six months a year and the other six months would be taken up by recording and hanging out. One of the sad aspects of it, and this includes more than just Janis, is the fact that she was recording for Columbia, which has very strict rules as to how, when, and where you can record. So if we don't have any more of Janis on record, it's because of that. Columbia only allows its artists to record in its own studios, with its own engineers handling the board.

She did a thing on the next Big Brother album, didn't she?

She sang a little background, a cameo role. Well, do you remember the Hells Angels dance in San Rafael at what is now Pepperland? Well, that was the scene. That was like her first gig out with the new band, and Big Brother was on the same bill. It was like a head to head confrontation scene. And so

everybody was drinking like mad, Janis was drinking Southern Comfort, I was drinking Benedictine and Brandy, and tequila and beer and the Hells Angels were all prodding everybody to get crazy. So I got on stage and I was drunk as a skunk, and a couple of nude people were dancing away and I was totally impervious to anything. I was just trying to do my best, and we played our asses off, down on one knee, raise up your right hand, you know, the whole thing. Played our asses off and then when it was over I collapsed. I had my old lady drive me home, I was totally wiped out.

Janis got up. She'd been drinking, she had a bottle up there, she was belting it, she'd just had a fight with a Hells Angel over the bottle of booze, the Hells Angel punched her and took the bottle and another Hells Angel jumped in—it was all real fucking crazy. She was up there singing and she knocked everybody out. She knocked herself out too; 'cause she collapsed, too. She took two steps off the stage and passed out. It was like one of those nights where everybody is going to outdo everybody else. But we were on the same stage with her. We did a thing with her in San Diego.

Sometimes it was easy. Around here it would have been easy for Big Brother and Janis to get on the same stage but to go into places that didn't know the bands, that just got their information out of the press, the star riff—we were in a very bad position there, Janis had cut us in half. She'd come on stage, we'd be doing a gig and she'd come up and stand around on stage and she'd sing a little bit in the background and occasionally at the Lion's Share she'd come and sit with the band.

I think that probably the most joyous time of her life would probably have gone down right after the album was finished; where she would have the chance to come home and hang out in a beautiful pad and all her friends would come by . . . that was in the works. I feel real protective about her —she was a real blues person.

She wanted to be cremated, and her family wants her buried. She didn't want a funeral and her family wants one. Also, she left $2500 for her good buddies to have a party. People are going to have to figure out who her good buddies are.

—October 29, 1970

ANOTHER CANDLE BLOWN OUT

BY RALPH J. GLEASON

My candle burns at both ends;
It will not last the night;
But, ah, my foes, and, oh, my friends
It gives a lovely light.
                    —Edna St. Vincent Millay

God knows, that blazing candle did cast a lovely light, even though from time to time when it flickered and the light dimmed, the looming face of tragedy appeared.

For Janis, gamin-faced, husky-voiced little girl lost, seemed to me from the moment I first saw her to have that fatal streak of tragedy present. And what's more, to know it.

Laughin' just to keep from crying.

It was just paralyzing to hear the radio bulletin that she was dead. Inevitable but paralyzing still when it happened. How could it be? Why?

And it makes no difference, really, what any inquest finds. She's dead and that's it, and the truth, which is sometimes much more difficult to see than the facts, ma'am, just the facts, is that she was driven to self-destruction by some demon deep within her from the moment she left that Texas high school where they had laughed at her.

She showed them, all right, she showed them plenty and the dues she paid to show them proved too much in the end.

Janis's effect on the San Francisco scene was like a time bomb or a depth charge. There was a long lag before it went off. She came up from Texas, a beatnik folk singer, and sang in the Coffee Gallery and the other crummy joints that were available at the end of the Beat era and just before the Haight blossomed so briefly only, like Janis, to self-destruct.

It wasn't until she came back from Texas with Chet and joined the band that she really hit, and what a hit it was. It took me a while to absorb it, but once that group got to you, they were a turn-on of magnificent proportions— much, much heavier than anything she ever got on record. That's why her own group, when she went out with it, was such a disappointment. Janis with Big Brother was magic, never mind that they played out of tune, never mind

any of the criticisms; over in the corner on the stage at the Avalon when she screamed, our hearts screamed with her. And when she stomped on that stage at Winterland (and stomped is the word) and shook her head and hollered, it was just simply unbelievable.

For all the notoriety (what feature writer could overlook a girl who insisted on drinking like an F. Scott Fitzgerald legend?), Janis's greatest moments came at Monterey, really, which were perhaps the finest moments that movement of which she was so integral a part has ever seen.

Janis did it three times at Monterey. She broke it up in the afternoon show and was brought back in the evening. They couldn't believe what they had seen. The rock set from Hollywood and New York, who had never heard of Janis Joplin nor of Big Brother and the Holding Company, got the hit of their lives that day. Her Monterey Pop appearance made her national news, the film made her national box office.

But the one I dug even more was three months later at the Monterey Jazz Festival (held in the same arena) when Janis came on at the afternoon blues show which featured B. B. King and T-Bone Walker, Clara Ward and Big Joe Turner.

There she was, this freaky-looking white kid from Texas on stage with all the hierarchy of the traditional blues world, facing an audience that was steeped in blues tradition, which was older than her ordinary audience and which had a built-in tendency to regard electric music as the enemy.

The first thing she did was to say "shit" and that endeared her right away. Then she stomped her foot and shook her hair and started to scream. They held still for a couple of seconds, but here and there in the great sunlit arena, longhairs started getting up and out into the aisles and stomping along with the band. By the end of the first number, the Monterey County Fairgrounds arena was packed with people writhing and twisting and snaking along in huge chains. It was an incredible sight. Nothing like it had ever happened before in the festival's ten years and nothing like it has happened since.

It was Janis's day, no doubt about it. She turned them on like they had not been turned on in years. Old and young, long hair or short, black or

white, they reacted like somebody had stuck a hot wire in their ass.

Janis had been scared silly before going on stage (I think she was scared silly every time she went on stage) and when she came off, she knew she had done it even though she was out of her mind with excitement. We had been filming for Educational Television that weekend and Janis's manager at the time, in a burst of paranoia still to be equaled, had refused to OK our filming Janis's performance. "Did you film it?" she asked, quivering, when she got off stage and I had to tell her "No." She was disappointed. She knew what it had been. And God knows, the world has less than it might have because we couldn't film that incredible performance.

There were so many, though. Everywhere, but especially in the city she had adopted. At Winterland and California Hall and the Old Fillmore and Fillmore West and the Avalon and all around Robin Hood's barn. But then Janis was really a part of the city when she was home. You'd see her anywhere, likely to pop up at a flick, in the park, at Enrico's. Anywhere. She dug it, and the city, with its tradition of eccentrics back to Emperor Norton, dug her.

Janis was a phenomenon, no question about it. Nobody else ever came close to doing what she did. The whole stance of American popular music has been to sound black, and generations of white girl singers, from Sophie Tucker to Dusty Springfield, have tried to do it. Some of them have been driven to as tragic an end as Janis in the attempt. But none of them, Peggy Lee, nobody, has ever made it in their own terms as a white girl singing black music to the degree Janis did.

It was only partly the voice and only partly the phrasing. It was, I am convinced, the concept. Janis was the very first white singer I ever saw who moved on stage with the music in a totally unselfconscious manner. She did not seem to *care* about anything but the music. And she conceived of it in different terms than did her predecessors, all of whom were trying to be blues singers of the Forties or Thirties or earlier. Janis was a blues singer of right now. And she took the blues, even the blues of ten or fifteen years ago, and made it immediate in its sound, by the way she propelled the words out of her mouth, by the way she shaped the sounds and by the volume she poured into it.

When she recorded that first time with Big Brother for Mainstream, she won my heart. I had said something about what an artistic crime it had been for Mainstream to make such a bad representation of what the band did. I met her a bit later in the dressing room at the Avalon. "Hey man, thanks for what you said about our shitty record," she said.

And her own albums on Columbia had their good and bad points too. When I first heard "Little Girl Blue" I didn't dig it at all because I felt Janis lacked something that was necessary for that jazz-bent number. But it haunts me now as a symbol of her loneliness, her despair, little girl lost in the big, wicked world.

She was impulsive, generous, softhearted, shy and determined. She had style and class and in a way she didn't believe it. What did she want? It was all there for her but something that she knew wasn't fated to happen. Many people loved her a very great deal, like many people loved Billie Holiday, but somehow that was not enough.

We'll never know and it doesn't matter, in a sense, because that brightly burning candle made an incredibly strong light in its brief life.

They heard Janis Joplin round the world, loud and clear, and they will continue to hear her. I am only sorry for those who never had the flash of seeing her perform.

Janis and Big Brother sang hymns at Monterey. It never seemed to me to be just music. I hope now that she's freed herself of that ball and chain, that she is at rest. She gave us a little piece of her heart and all of her soul every time she went on stage.

Monterey, 1967. Otis, Jimi, Brian, Janis. Isn't that enough?

Little girl blue, with the floppy hats and the brave attempt to be one of the guys. She took a little piece of all of us with her when she went. She was beautiful. That's not corny. It's true.

—*October 29, 1970*

INTERVIEW WITH COUNTRY JOE McDONALD

They wanted to see her shoot up, they wanted to see her get loud, they wanted to see her scream and yell and screech about, and to do that to that extreme was to like deny the fact that she had a really soft side to her, really tender side to her. She was very concerned about her family, about her little brother. She wanted to—I know that she wanted to have children that she wanted to someday be married. But I think if she had lived, if this accident hadn't happened, she would have mellowed out, she would have really mellowed out. In, you know, two, three, four years.

Do you think it was an accident on any more than a surface level? What you seem to be saying was that it was almost inevitable, that you half expected it.

Some people need a lot of convincing that love is around them and she—her excuses were running out. Her game was running out because her dreams were all coming true. I mean she was getting rich, she was getting famous, she could have anything she wanted to and the only thing left for her to have was love, to give it and take it.

But instead of that she would feel sorry for herself and she would shoot up, and what you're supposed to think is poor Janis—poor, poor Janis, she is shooting up. Well, that's a junky game that you can play and there have been people all around me, and we all know people that have played that game and lost. It seems like there are some people, it's like a genetic trait that they want to kill themselves. And she . . . I do believe, though, I do believe that, well . . . I met her at Shea Stadium about a month and a half or two months before at a big peace rally that she brought her band to play at, which is a strange thing for her to do, a political thing, you know. But I think she was growing up. She was really drunk, getting really morose, a typical kind of drunk, you know, saying that she couldn't help what she did, that she was a slave to the audience, her fans, and that they wanted her to be this way so that was the way she was acting.

But with me she always seemed to be honest, and I picked up that her anger was turning into sadness. Which is like a real breakthrough, because when you're angry, you think everyone else is to blame. But when you finally come to the conclusion, when it starts to break through that no one is to blame for what you're feeling, that there's just no one to blame, that certain things happen to everybody and you can hang on to the resentment as long as you want to but it's going to hang you up and you have to let go of it, then you have to confront yourself and accept the fact that you're really unhappy. And I think she was beginning to confront that. And she had this boyfriend and she was talking about getting married which is a very, very far out thing for her to do, and a very feminine thing, for her to decide to get married.

You mentioned Janis. How close were you to her and how did you first meet her?—that sort of thing.

Well, I first met her because we were playing a gig with Big Brother at the Golden Sheaf Bakery in Berkeley, which was one of those production enterprises that never quite worked out—they put on about three concerts. Anyway, we were playing there with them. Country Joe and the Fish, and I met her that night. I was on acid that night and I was just very quiet and she was her usual gregarious self and we just talked a couple times. Then we played together at the Avalon Ballroom, I think, one night, and then we just started going together and it lasted I guess about three months, four months. It was the Haight-Ashbury, we were playing concerts in the park and stuff like that, before the big flood. Janis was living on Ashbury.

What did you like about her?

I thought she had a nice sense of humor, and she was smart, and I thought she was pretty. She was just very interesting and we seemed to get along very well. Same kind of personality, we're both Capricorns, both singers. We got along on almost everything except—well, it was a strange combination because I was into psychedelic drugs and she wasn't into psychedelic drugs.

Not at all?

No. I think she might have had acid; no, I don't think she had acid at all then. She had been through a lot of speed but she wasn't shooting anything when I was with her. It was a very lovely time, actually, for everybody—carefree, no pressure—everyone was just becoming famous. I was into some political trips and she wasn't into political trips at all, she was suspicious of them. That was one big thing that we used to argue about.

She thought it was pointless?

Well, she thought that you should take care of yourself and not worry about everybody else. Basically she was as right as I was right at that time, we both were very extreme. She felt that she didn't need anybody to take care of her at all or to help her out or teach her anything, and I felt that I needed everybody and everything to help me out and teach me everything. At that time I was splitting up all my copyright royalties with the band, and she thought that I was insane for doing it. And it turned out that I *was* pretty insane for doing it.

And things just broke down with you the way they do with most people?

Yeah, it was just, I don't know, just one day I said we're not getting along so well and she said yeah, I know it, and I said I guess I'll leave and she said yeah, I guess so. It was a very casual sort of thing. We were both into being with the band, you know, the bands were really tight at that time. It was hard to get it on with somebody else. The most serious commitment that anybody had was their thing.

Did you see her much after that?

A little bit, but we didn't work together, so it just kinda spread itself apart. And then after we had been apart for like about a month or so she said, "You know, before we get too far apart, would you do me a favor and write a song for me?" And so I wrote the song "Janis" which turned out to be a really pretty song. She was at one time going to sing it with the band but the band was into such a heavy trip that it was impossible for her to do it.

Different kind of music, you mean.

Yeah, heavy, really hard rock and stuff. She had a really pretty ballad voice and never really got a chance to use it until the last record; but I think her voice was really blown out on the last record. She really can't reach the high notes very well, and a lot of quality seems to be gone.

How did you find out that she had died?

I was in Chile—Santiago, Chile—working on this movie with Saul Landau. I had only been there two days when I got a call from the States saying that she had died. I think it was always—I think everybody knew that she was going to die or that possibly she would die and it was a toss-up. It seemed to me it was a time when she was just beginning to confront some of her fears about herself so that she wouldn't have to use drugs anymore. Life was mellow enough where her dreams were coming true and she was having to face up to the reality that she was a woman and needed some love. She had to deal with the conflict of love which was a hard one for her to deal with. Anybody who is using hard drugs, I think, is experiencing a conflict of love—she continued to confuse drugs and love.

I was in Chile and I couldn't quite get it together, I was sort of in shock about it. And then, about a week later, a very strange thing happened. We moved to Copiapo, Chile, which is a really small little town, only about 70,000 people in it, and the principal industry there is mining. A lot of the people there have never been out of Copiapo, it's a very provincial, small little town and the men on their days off go and drink beer and they have a lot of Catholic churches. So we were filming in the town square. They were going to stage a mock rally of the left wing because this was the time of Allende and it was a movie about modern revolution in Chile. But the principals in the movie had gotten stuck on the road so they weren't there to make the shot, they were like an hour late, and there was a big crowd of people that had gathered around because they had been told to come and pretend like they were a crowd at a demonstration.

So I went up and did a set. I didn't speak any Spanish and they didn't speak any English—I've been in a lot of strange situations playing and so I just thought OK, here's another weird one—I started doing my regular songs and then all of a sudden I thought, hey, I'm going to do "Janis." [Joe, frowning, his eyes straight ahead, starts nervously picking at his fingernails.] I sang it and it was just somehow very—I've thought about it a lot after that; Saul was there watching me do it and he knew that I sang it for her wherever it was that she was or if she *was* anymore, but the song was there and the people were there and the people didn't know it was Janis Joplin—it was a heavy kind of sad, sentimental, kind of lovely sort of thing. Just sitting there, they had this one microphone propped up on the chair and I just sang the song. It was very far out, very surreal. Somehow I was the wrong person to be in that place, it was the wrong time, it was the wrong song, but they all listened to the song and applauded afterwards and it somehow seemed just perfect.

When I came back and I started reading all the *Rolling Stone* articles about Janis, someone was quoted as saying one of the wonderful things about Janis is that she was just one of the guys. She just wanted to be one of the guys. I know that's true about her, but I think that was one of the things that drove her to drugs. On the one hand people wanted her to be a sex symbol and on the other hand she wasn't the conventional sex symbol in any kind of way. Her bone structure was wrong, the way she acted was wrong—they wanted her to be Billie Holiday and she wasn't Billie Holiday at all because Billie Holiday was very very feminine and dainty and Janis wasn't at all.

I think it was that aspect of her personality that caused her to shoot. I mean she was a woman and she was a very feminine woman. I don't know what happened to her in Texas in her childhood, but I got the feeling that she was just the wrong person in the wrong place and got treated in the wrong way. She was real, she was a real woman and people kept treating her like one of the guys. They wanted to see her shoot up.

—May 27, 1971

BANDS DUST TO DUST

BY TONY GLOVER

MINNEAPOLIS—On their recent "farewell" tour, Big Brother and the Holding Company even got as far as Minneapolis. Outside, the hippie-heads are floating towards the theatre. The new wave here is dropouts with bread, and you can see it on their backs; expensive patterned shirts, boots, and pseudo-Joplin shawls, even a Ken Kesey fan who's wearing a flag as a cape. Most all of the tickets were sold in advance, so there are hawkers and hustlers there, everybody trying to score. For Minneapolis this is more than a concert, it's a gathering of the faithful, to share a trip together.

The main trip is Janis Joplin, the

little girl with the Big voice, all the way from Port Arthur to Life magazine, famous for a life style as much as a music. One critic said that hearing her sing when she was in top form was "like getting laid, lovingly and well." I remember a record store salesman telling of a middle-aged cat with an armful of classical albums coming to the desk while *Cheap Thrills* was playing, nodding towards it and saying, "Janis Joplin?"

It seems that Big Brother has surfaced, so the audience at the concert was a mixture of those who were, or knew someone who was, at Monterey, and those who follow the mass-media concept of current life scenes.

My friend John, the road manager, shows up in a Hertz station wagon at 7:15, he's dropped the band in backstage, past the guard, and the Guthrie Theatre people get uptight when John asks them to let the band in the front way.

"They'll have to come around back," a turtle neck medallion says firmly.

"Well, I'd rather not have them walk all that way with their instruments and accumulating people, you understand," John says in that mixture of patience and exasperation common to road managers. There are a few words exchanged, but the hassle is settled when the band comes walking in thru the auditorium, and then heads downstairs for the dressing rooms. The equipment has already been set up on stage and David Getz heads immediately for his drums, knocking out a few tentative riffs.

The rest of the band stalks into the dressing rooms, past a rack in the hall full of costumes from some Shakespeare thing that had been running at the theatre. "It's cold in here!" somebody complains, and John goes to see about shutting the air conditioning off.

Janis is like her pictures, only more so, regal and funky at the same time. She spies a cape and hat, swashbuckling style, and tries it on in the mirror. "Wow man, I look like a goddam king!" she shouts in triumph. She finds a sword and waves it around menacingly. "Okay varlet," she commands imperiously to the air. "Bring me thirteen pretty boys and line 'em up aganist this wall, RIGHT NOW!" On the table in her dressing room is the standard fifth of Southern Comfort, waiting.

In the other dressing room James Gurley is playing some flamenco runs, getting loose. On stage Sam Andrew is setting his guitar level.

A very neat young man with umbrella in hand appears in front of Janis and hands her a copy of his local magazine, he's talking fast and smooth. Janis peers out from under her borrowed hat:

"No man, I don't do interviews anymore," she says. "They were all beginning to sound alike, so what's the point? Talk to the band . . ." He adjusts his umbrella and approaches the others. Janis smiles and shakes her head.

The audience is filing in. One can hear the rustle and murmur over the monitor speakers near the ceiling. John bustles past at controlled road-manager urgency. Peter Albin asks what the sound is like. "Don't worry man," John answers. "It's the best you ever heard. Segovia would play here without a PA, right?" Peter nods. "It's like a recording trip, huh?" John agrees and Peter goes next door and plugs his bass into the tuning amp and proceeds to tighten up on it.

Janis is out in the hallway making *en garde* thrusts with the sword when the backstage cop comes in. His eyes widen a little, then he grins slightly and goes to see that everything is on the up and up. It is, and he goes away. Janis looks like a little kid who's been caught carving her initials in a desk for a moment, then she remembers who she is and laughs.

The band comes onstage and finaltunes in the darkness. Then! the spotlight hits the door, and Janis strolls out, thunderous applause accompanying her as she makes her way to the mike. Just as she reaches it there's a resounding crash from the band, and they're into "Piece of My Heart."

Janis screams, moans and coos lyrics, stomping and posing like an imperious whore, stroking her mike, whipping her hair around . . . the audience is rolling around in the palm of her hand. The band takes long instrumental breaks, more freak-rock than blues (including James eating his guitar), but Janis and the band come right together and drive each other further. At one point the top of the mike stand comes loose and it's flopping around. Janis tries to fix it.

"Got a screwdriver?" she asks the

band. "Or a dime?" Nobody does. "Throw change," she says half-sarcastically to the audience and it rings down on the stage. She picks out a dime and gets the stand straightened out. Into more sounds, and after one heavy number she's out of breath, panting. Peter Albin, the bassman, says "Now we're doing an imitation of Lassie." The audience laughs, but Janis flashes him a look and mutters something. One more song and the first half is over.

Janis is on a chair backstage, screaming at John: "Man, he called me a dog! On stage, in front of everybody. I don't have to take that shit!"

"The audience thought it was funny," John says.

"Well, I don't, goddamit!" She was in a total rage; vibrations are what they call bad. The band has been on the road, jammed in planes and hotels and dressing rooms together for five days straight. Nerves wear thin.

On top of that, Janis had shortly before given the band notice that she was splitting to go solo, although it had not yet then been publicly announced. In the dressingroom, Peter is muttering: "Man she don't have to come down on me like that onstage, she's got no right to do that!"

"Listen," John is back and forth trying to cool it out, "you both said something you shouldn't have, but why not forget it? It's been a very groovy evening so far, let's try and keep it that way, huh?"

More snarls from both sides, and Janis demands a cup of whiskey. Umbrella man comes back with a photographer. He hangs up his coat, wipes his brow carefully and tells the cameraman what to shoot, meanwhile asking things like "Who is Janis's favorite poet?"

"Ask *her*," is the reply. Tension is heavy right up to when the stage man calls "places." "People are getting impatient," he says tiredly: "It's all right," says David, "they're as patient as the day is long." The door is closed and John is reasoning with them.

Remember, fame is a hard trip. From a backup band playing second bills to heavy gigs for heavy bread in less than a year takes its toll in more ways than one.

First there's the continual pressure to be great; no matter where you are or how you feel, you have to be right on—or the word goes out that you've gone lame. And the fans; everybody wants to turn you on to their trip—which is fine for *them,* but carrying on every night with different people in a different town can bring you down.

And the downtown press, coming on all blasé and bitter—"Well you look like freaks to me, but I got this assignment, what'd you say your name was?" The questions, the same old questions, and they all should be answered just like it was the first time you ever were asked.

Add the straights hard-timing you in the hotels, the airports, the restaurants, the toilets, count up all the hours of sleep you'll never get back, all the rotten meals, all the Muzak, in the elevators, in the lobbies, and it's hard to see why everybody doesn't just flip out completely.

Fame and fortune is no easy ride. Just get on board for a few months and see where your head is at. But until then watch out, "lest you wind up on this road . . ." So the atmosphere is a bit explosive.

The band is onstage, but no Janis. I wonder if she's decided not to go on—finally somebody calls out "Janis, come out and play," and she makes her way slowly onstage. But she's professional thru and thru, nobody can tell there's been a hassle. She wails thru the old and new numbers, her back to Peter. They finish with the classic "Ball and Chain." Janis is in cathartic agony as she wraps herself around the song—she whips the mike out of the stand and it topples over. The song closes with her voice solo, and as she sobs out the last note she tosses the mike to the floor, drained.

And it's over, but the audience is standing and clapping and clapping. So the band comes back with the uptempo "Down On Me." Then it's really over and the audience, fulfilled, streams out, some heading for the backstage door to wait for the band, others to gather out front and rap about who's doing what where and for how much.

In the dressing rooms the scene is bad, if not worse. The words are the kind that have to do with deeper things than the hassle itself. John is trying to get everybody together to escape back to the hotel. Finally it's decided to use the front door because there are less people there. Janis is tired, depressed and doesn't want to talk to

anybody. The wagon pulls up, she walks out to it. The kids there hardly notice, they're looking for the band as a unit.

"Have you ever been in love?" Janis asks me, stepping in the wagon. "Well, I haven't" she says, "that's why these hassles are so bad—the only love I have is with the audience, and that's my whole life. Man I ain't got anything else!"

The band finally arrives, signs a few autographs and splits. There's a whole little train of cars and bikes, including a chick with long blonde hair in a VW, and she's right on the bumper of the wagon all the way. John makes some half-hearted attempts to lose her, but she ends up right in front of the hotel with the band. She gets out, and poses calmly against her car, looking as though she's been there all night, and *Wham!* she's in earnest conversation with Sam.

There's a party up, the band is going, but Janis cuts back to her room, all alone, not a word to anybody. John shrugs: "That's the way it goes down sometimes," he says.

—*November 23, 1968*

———

Two details which should be corrected in the following article: Janis's second group was never called The Janis Joplin Revue, which would have been an ego trip for her; also she was not staying at the Lorraine Motel, where Martin Luther King was shot.

THE MEMPHIS DEBUT

BY STANLEY BOOTH

"Janis," I said, "I'm going to write a little something for Rolling Stone *about your new band's debut in Memphis, and—"*

"Rolling Stone? Those shits! They don't know what's happening, they're out in San Francisco feeling smug because they think they're where it's at. This is where it's at, Memphis!"

MEMPHIS—People say that Janis Joplin is the best white female blues singer of our time, but what other white girl sings blues? The remarkable thing

about Janis Joplin is that she is a *real* blues singer, in "our" time, when imitations are good enough for most people. She has, like all true originals, a strong sense of tradition, and Memphis is the blues singers' La Scala—the Gateway to the Mississippi Delta, where Furry Lewis, Mississippi John Hurt, Memphis Minnie, Gus Cannon, Butterfly Washington, Howlin' Wolf, Sonny Boy Williamson, Bukka White, John Lee Hooker, Muddy Waters, and B. B. King made their earlier recordings; where Johnny Cash, Jerry Lee Lewis, Carl Perkins, Roy Orbison, and Elvis Presley made their yellow Sun records, and where, in recent years, Otis Redding, Booker T. and the MG's, Wilson Pickett, Sam and Dave, Eddie Floyd, and Rufus and Carla Thomas have recorded their great soul music. (Aretha Franklin cuts in New York, but with musicians flown up from Memphis.)

So it was important to Janis Joplin, the only outside act invited to the Second Annual Stax/Volt Yuletide Thing, that she do well. And did she? Backstage after it was all over, she said, "At least they didn't throw things." Janis Joplin died in Memphis, but it wasn't her fault.

The Yuletide Thing was scheduled for Saturday night, December 21, at the Memphis Mid-South Coliseum. Miss Joplin had left Big Brother and the Holding Company and was rehearsing with a new group of musicians but not until Wednesday, December 18, when Mike Bloomfield came to San Francisco, acting on orders from manager Albert Grossman to help with arrangements and pull the act together, did the Janis Joplin Revue achieve any sort of unity. They rehearsed on Wednesday and Thursday in San Francisco, and on Friday afternoon in the B studio at the Stax/Volt Recording Company in Memphis. They had come to Memphis a day early to attend a Christmas cocktail party at the home of Stax president Jim Stewart.

It was the smallest and most prestigious Memphis Sound party of recent years, a Stax family affair with just a few carefully selected outside guests. There were tables laden with great bowls of fat pink shrimp, chafing dishes with bacon-wrapped chicken livers, all sorts of sandwiches dyed red and green for Christmas, and plate after plate of olives, candies, and other trifles. In one corner a large Christmas tree was standing, its colored lights blinking off and on. Some of the guests were sitting on the leopard-print couches, some on the thick red rug. Isaac Hayes and David Porter, authors of "Soul Man," "Hold On, I'm Comin'," and other Sam and Dave hits, were there, Hayes dressed all in black, Porter in red. Steve Cropper, Stax producer and MG's guitarist, was wearing a black cut-velvet suit and green ruffled shirt. (He plans, by the way, to start work early in 1969 on his long-awaited guitar album, which will probably include "What Becomes of the Broken-Hearted," "Soul Strut," and, no kidding, "Green Tambourine.") Donald "Duck" Dunn, the MG's wonderful red-bearded bass player, refused the bar's fine whiskey and drank Budweiser. "I can drink this till nine in the mornin', and I can't that other," Duck explained. " 'Course, I'll feel this till nine tomorrow night."

Into this pleasant scene Janis and her band descended, making hardly a ripple. One of the outside guests, somebody's wife, did discover, not who Janis was, but that she was *somebody,* and asked for an autograph. "It's for my son, Barney," the woman said. "That's B-a-r-n-e-y." Janis signed a slip of paper and gave it to the woman, who was not satisfied. "No," she said, "It's got to say, 'To Barney,' B-a-r-n-e-y." Janis took the paper and started again to write. "That's B-a-r-n-e-y, Barney," the woman said.

"I *know*," Janis told her, "how to spell Barney."

Memphis had not known what to expect of Janis Joplin, this "hippie queen." There was some fear that she might turn out to be blatantly unprofessional, as so many people are in contemporary popular music. It was a relief, then, backstage the next night at the Yuletide Thing, to see that she was wearing makeup and a cerise jersey pants-suit with bursts of cerise feathers at the cuffs. She looked like a girl who was ready to go out and entertain the people.

Mike Bloomfield had come into town and spent the day working with the band, and Albert Grossman himself was on hand to see how things went. They might have gone beautifully. The Janis Joplin Revue was set to appear after all the other acts except Johnny Taylor, a minor Stax artist whose recent million-selling single, "Who's

Making Love," earned him the closing spot.

I was in a corridor backstage, talking with Mike Bloomfield, Steve Cropper, and Duck Dunn, when the first act, the re-formed Bar-Kays (four of the instrumental group's original members died the year before in the airplane crash that also killed Otis Redding) came out of their dressing room wearing zebra-striped flannel jumpsuits. Bloomfield's eyes widened. It was the first sign of the cultural gap that was to increase as the evening progressed.

The thing is, a stage act in Memphis, Tennessee (or, as the famous Stax marquee puts it, "Soulsville, U.S.A.") is not the same as a stage act in San Francisco, Los Angeles, or New York. These days a lot of people think if a fellow comes on stage wearing black vinyl pants, screams that he wants to fuck his poor old mother, then collapses, that's a stage act; but in Memphis, if you can't do the Sideways Pony, you just don't have a stage act.

The Bar-Kays did the Pony, they boogalooed, stomped, hunched, screwed each other with guitars, did the 1957 Royales act at triple the 1957 speed, were loud, lewd, and a general delight. After three songs they were followed by Albert King and his funky blues, but they came back, now dressed all in red, to boogaloo behind the Mad Lads, William Bell, Judy Clay, and Rufus and Carla Thomas. Rufus, "The Dog," and his beautiful daughter, who was wearing a rhinestone-encrusted turquoise gown, sang "The Night Time Is the Right Time," and did a dance that stopped just short of incest. Members of Janis Joplin's Revue watched from the wings, shaking their heads.

After a brief intermission, Booker T. and the MG's appeared and played, as they always do, impeccably. They accompanied the next act, the Staple Singers, who did "For What It's Worth," and a very moving "Ghetto." Then Eddie Floyd, who is not, by a long shot, Otis Redding, but is still a very good soul singer, came on and got the biggest audience response of the night. He opened with "Knock On Wood," and during his next song, "I Never Found a Girl," had dozens of girls coming down to the stage to touch his hand. If Janis had come on directly after he left the stage, she might have got the kind of reception she wanted. But that's not the way it happened.

When the Bar-Kays jump around in their zebra suits, and Carla Thomas does the Dog with her daddy, they are hamboning; but then so is Frank Zappa hamboning when he belches into the microphone at the Fillmore. The crowd at the Fillmore, East or West, expects to see a band shove equipment around the stage for ten minutes or more, "getting set up"—not being show-biz, in that context, is accepted show-biz practice.

But in Memphis, this is not what the people come to see. The warmth that Eddie Floyd's appearance had generated was dispelled while Janis' band put their instruments in order. She planned to do three songs and then encore with her specialties, "Ball and Chain," and "Piece of My Heart." Obviously she did not realize that about half the audience, the black people, had no idea who Janis Joplin was, and the other half, mostly teenaged whites, had never heard her do anything except her two best-known songs.

She opened with "Raise Your Hand," an Eddie Floyd song, and followed it with the Bee-Gees' "To Love Somebody." She sang well, in full control of her powerful voice.

The band was not together, but they all seemed to be excellent musicians, and one could predict that, given sufficient rehearsal time, they would make a great back-up band for Janis, if they did not have one basic flaw; none of them plays blues. They come from the Electric Flag, the Paupers, the Chicago Loop, and one is left over from Big Brother and the Holding Company. They can all play, but not blues, and who is there to teach them? Certainly not Mike Bloomfield, whose music, like Paul Butterfield's, is a pastiche of incompatible styles. One Memphis musician suggested that three months at Hernando's Hideaway, the Club Paradise, or any of the Memphis night spots where they frisk you before you go in, might give them an inkling as to what the blues is about. Failing that, Janis might start over with some musicians who know already how to do the Sideways Pony.

When she finished her third song and started to leave the stage, there was almost no applause, and so, of course, no encore. A few people went backstage, where everyone from the Revue was in shock, staring at the walls, and tried to tell Janis that she was not to blame for what happened. She had sung well, and the rest had been beyond her control. But she wasn't having any of it, and soon she went back to her room at the Lorraine Motel, where Martin Luther King had been killed, and where B. B. King and a lot of other blues singers had spent unhappy nights before her.

—February 1, 1969

JANIS: THE JUDY GARLAND OF ROCK AND ROLL?

BY PAUL NELSON

NEW YORK—When Janis Joplin danced on stage in front of her new, as-yet-unnamed, six-piece band at the Fillmore East February 11 and 12, she seemed to have victory within her grasp. How could she miss? There had been a "sound test" for the band (as road manager John Cooke put it) in Rindge, New Hampshire, a "preview" in Boston—but this was Opening Night, the Big Debut, and the city's rockers has been busy working themselves into a lather for days. All four performances were sold out, and ticket scalpers roamed along Second Avenue offering paradise at prices that would have been out of line for a kilo of hash.

Tuesday's opening night crowd had more than a hint of uptown prosperity to it. Affluent reporters from Time, Life, Look, Newsweek, and other bastions of slick-paper supremacy laid claim to most of the complimentary tickets, while those hardy souls from the lower echelon rock press either stood outside in the slush, their faces pressed against the glass, or somehow got past the door only to huddle together in the lobby and standing-room areas to look in vain for an empty seat. Mike Wallace and a CBS television crew were on hand documenting the building's events for a March 4 segment of *60 Minutes* to be called, with true media irony, "Carnegie Hall for Kids."

Through the balloon-filled air, the Grateful Dead, the "other half" of an all-San Francisco program, started to play "Good Morning, Little Schoolgirl."

And play they did—one of those wonderful, comfortable, one-long-song sets that went uninterrupted for close to an hour and actually managed to neutralize much of the inherent tension by turning the concert into something not unlike a feebie in the park or a pleasant party at somebody's home.

The band played well—but, more important, gave New York audiences something of the idea of rock as a relaxed and relaxing way of life, not as a sporadic series of super-hypes for super-groups. There were no artifically induced high points or low points, no cream-in-your-jeans climax—instead, a steady stream of satisfying music which simply went on until it stopped.

Nonprofessional response to the buildup was interesting. One long-term Joplin fanatic, a young man named Ronnie Finkelstein, approached the Fillmore with ecstasy and hurried to his seat just as the Grateful Dead began their set. "I found them original and satisfying," he said. "I wanted Janis, though.

"I rushed back when Bill Graham— the dirty capitalist!—introduced my girl. The band futzed around for about five minutes, and then, with a short brass intro, Janis appeared out of nowhere. In a cape-gown sort of thing, she danced for a minute, then threw off the cape to reveal her famous shoulder-strap pants outfit. Was I excited!"

Another admirer put it even more succinctly. "I've had a hard-on since four o'clock this afternoon waiting for this."

This consisted of an incredibly nervous Janis Joplin—hair flying, long fingers showing white clenching a hand mike—in front of her new group: Sam Andrew from Big Brother and the Holding Company, lead guitar; Terry Clements, sax; Richard Kermode, organ; Roy Markowitz, drums; Terry Hensley, trumpet; and a temporary bass player, Keith Cherry (ex-Pauper Brad Campbell is expected to come down from Canada to join the band as a permanent member as soon as he can get a work permit).

The first song made a number of things both painfully and delightfully clear. The potential to become a genuinely great rock singer is still there, but so are the infamous and disheartening Joplin tendencies toward vocal overkill. Indeed, Janis doesn't so much sing a song as to strangle it to death right in front of you. It's an exciting, albeit, grisly, event to behold. But it would seem to belong more to the realm of carnival exhibition than musical performance.

Kenneth Tynan once wrote of Richard Burton: "Without flow or pattern, he jerked from strangled sobs to harsh, intolerant roars, lacking a middle register for contemplation. It was all stubbornly conscientious, rising to something like grandeur in moments of decision, but I couldn't help noting that absence of . . . the essential." The same words might almost apply to Joplin: her glory is that she doesn't lack even the essential; her tragedy is that, as yet, she has been unable to use it.

On the first number, the band made all local stops, while Janis was an express. The singing and playing simply failed to mesh, Joplin constantly projecting and the group continually receding. Between verses, the vocalist as dancer seemed more a constrained Radio City Rockette than a free-form blues singer. Every movement was stiff and preordained.

The applause was respectful. People seemed to be biding their time, waiting for the big explosion. Janis and the band plowed into the second song, a Nick Gravenites composition, and made it sound a smudged carbon copy of the first. Any sense of pace was forgotten. The audience began to pall. Joplin reached for her bottle of booze, a trademark which had been placed proudly on top of an amplifier with all of the deliberate care inherent in the planting of a religious symbol.

Things started to go better. "Maybe," an old Chantells' signature tune from the late Fifties, was good and hard, and "Summertime," born of *Cheap Thrills* but now instrumentally processed through Ars Nova and Blood, Sweat and Tears, brought with it flowers, affection, a watermelon rasp, some sneaky CBS cameramen, and a more appreciative response from admirers. Janis swayed a bit, rubbed her head fetchingly, and hitched up her pants with a jump.

Robin and Barry Gibb's "To Love Somebody" was rendered needlessly grotesque as Joplin ran through her rapidly depleting bagful of mannerisms in a desperate attempt to inject even more meaningfulness into the song by almost literally wiping up the floor with it. Then, a fast one, written by the group, which Janis said she wanted to call "Jazz for the Jack-offs." Again, the local-express syndrome, with a real credibility gap developing between star and support.

Came the highlight of the new act: Joplin's moving and only slightly over-ripe singing of a beautiful new Nick Gravenites song, "Work Me, Lord." Empathy and art formed a strong partnership at this point, and passion, throughout the evening so misused and purposeless, finally found a home in spiritual rock.

It is difficult to imagine a Bob Dylan or a John Lennon peppering an interview with constant nervous interjections of "Hey, I've never sung so great. Don't you think I'm singing better? Well, Jesus fucking Christ, I'm really better, believe me." But Janis seems that rare kind of personality who lacks the essential self-protective distancing that a singer of her fame and stature would appear to need.

One gets the alarming feeling that Joplin's whole world is precariously balanced on what happens to her musically—that the necessary degree of honest cynicism needed to survive an all-media assault may be buried too far under an immensely likeable but tremendously underconfident naivete.

She knows the band isn't together yet. Haven't worked together long enough—"Hey, it takes longer than a couple of weeks to get loose, to be really *tight*, to *push*. But conceptually I like it, and I think I'm singing better than I ever, ever did." This is what Janis Joplin *wants*, this band, these songs, all of it. "I mean, I really dig what I'm doing, but I just wish the band would push as hard as I am. Hey, I'm the lead, you know—but they're hanging back way too far for me."

It all takes time, she knows. Janis wants to sing and she wants other people in the band to sing, too. You get a bunch of musicians together so everybody can contribute to the final product, make it something larger than the sum. "Trouble is, we haven't really had a chance to get into each other yet."

"It's going to get better. She's sure it's going to get better. Like maybe she'll add a new cat next week—"great big ugly spade cat." He blows baritone and drums like Buddy Miles. "He's really *heavy*. I really need somebody to push, you know. There's really not

enough push in the band yet."

The band's got an even dozen songs together now. Not enough repertoire yet. But Nick Gravenites has been a big help. "Isn't his 'Work Me Lord' beautiful? Oh, man—whew! Man, I love that guy. His songs really *say* something."

Clive (Davis, president of Columbia Records) isn't hassling her to record right away, and it's just as well, Janis says. She doesn't understand people recording before they've had a chance to work at it. "Hey, I want to play a little more, I want to gig a little bit so that the tunes get together before I make a record."

Janis exudes several things at once: that the act is going fine right now; that it's not so fine; that it's going to get better; that, despite herself, there's the terror that it might *not*, unless something happens.

She's looking for a cat to be musical director, knows she doesn't know enough to do it herself. Somebody to pull it all together. Like Michael Bloomfield. Everybody's doing arrangements now and . . . it isn't working. Maybe that will have to come first before a new name for the group can be chosen. "I want a name that implies a band but has the person's name in it, right? Like the Buddy Miles Express. That has an identity to it. We were thinking," she laughs, "of Janis and the Joplinaires—ha!" Except that isn't what the band is. What is the band? Too soon to say.

"Well, people say that I'm singing great, man. The whole San Francisco scene, which I was afraid might be a little pissed at me for officially disclaiming the familial San Francisco rock thing, has been fine. Jerry Garcia [of the Grateful Dead] told me that I made him cry. The Dead have been so good to me, man. They're so warm and everything. I really needed that because of the pressure—I've been really scared because this is *important* to me.

"The kids—well, they're missing the familiar tunes. You know how audiences are. And I really want to do the new songs. I don't want to have to get up there and sing 'Down on Me' when I'm eighty years old. The reason I did this was so that I could keep on moving. Once I get the new tunes on a record, then the kids won't mind."

It will all be better then.

Doing the *60 Minutes* segment had

been really funny, Janis said she just laughed all the time at the media and the Big Build-Up she had gotten. It was too much to take seriously. "It's *surreal*. It's got nothing to do with me, really. I'm beginning to be able to cope with it. I don't believe it, you know—I mean, you can't." One thing you've got to be sure about, she thinks, is that you don't start believing you are worth all that attention. Janis laughed.

So the CBS *60 Minutes* crew had come the first night, set up with the band, and Janis—"I was really goofed at the time," she explains—told Mike Wallace: "Listen, man, if I start saying something you don't like, just scream '*Fuck*' because they'll have to take it out of the TV thing." If he asked a dumb question she'd do the same.

There sat Mike Wallace, cool and urbane, asking Janis Joplin something like, "Can a white man sing the blues?" "I just looked at the camera and said, 'Fuck.' I did the interview, but I don't remember it, being stoned."

Janis Joplin and her group played their first official gig at the Second Annual Stax/Volt Yuletide Thing in Memphis on December 21. Since then, the band's personnel has changed somewhat because one musician was drafted (the FBI took him away) and another, Marc Doubleday, decided he didn't want to go on the road.

Before the February 11 and 12 concerts at the Fillmore East, the group played in Rindge, New Hampshire, February 8 and at the Boston Music Hall February 9. Road manager John Cooke refers to the Rindge date as a "sound test," Boston as a "preview," and Fillmore East as "opening night." The band will tour the East for a month, rehearsing weekdays, gigging weekends, then back to San Francisco for a couple of weeks, then to Europe for a month—possibly to do a show in London with the Hells Angels.

Janis had thought the Fillmore East "opening" had gone well—"I'm really doing good," she thought—but the audience reaction had been decidedly mixed.

The kid who'd kept that hard-on all that while thought Janis was the greatest thing he'd ever seen, and didn't want to say any more than that. But Ronnie Finkelstein liked her better with Big Brother. Ronnie thought she was flaunting her sexuality and that altogether it was a vulgar display. "Her thing now is showboating. Her dancing was a drag. Everything sounded like a big put-on." An ex-worshiper, art director Gene Mallard, felt that success most definitely *had* spoiled Janis Joplin. This new thing was a brassy burlesque show—the old hypnoticism was gone—there was an air of boredom. "Miss Superstar and her group," said Mallard, "are just another put-together plasticized show."

—*March 15, 1969*

JANIS AND LONDON COME TOGETHER

BY JONATHAN COTT AND DAVID DALTON

"WHAT IS *that?*" asked Janis, looking out of her hotel window. "It looks like a hill with a house on top of it." "That's the Albert Hall, baby," somebody explained.

Janis turned that hill into a Volcano at her concert here on the 21st of April, inciting the 6,000 odd fans to shake it up, to dig themselves. ("You're looking good" Janis said to the audience and herself during a break for champagne and they shrieked back the compliment.) Janis breathed life into the Transylvanian bloodstream of hip London, woke up Love's Body asleep in Fashion's winding street. California does not travel well, and music is mainly an intellectual trip in London (as witness Cream's farewell concert when their fans behaved like an enthusiastic audience at a classical concert), but Janis did it like no-one since Jimi Hendrix (and ecstasy is a habit for Jimi); she brought the house down.

Janis functions on a direct charge, and the audience were behind her from the first note. They wanted her to take them away on her voice and body, riding through "Maybe," "Combination of the Two," "Summertime," "Work Me Lord," "Ball and Chain," as if she were a souped up Harley Davidson. The group backing her had the same lineup as at the New York concert: guitar, sax, trumpet, organ, bass, and drums. They were tight and kept a good balance in relation to Janis's voice, never drowning her out.

The Albert Hall looks like a gigantic Victorian mausoleum inside, and recently it looks even more surreal, with a fleet of "flying saucers" hung from the roof to baffle the notoriously bad acoustics. They look like grey loaves flying in a Magritte painting. Eric Clapton and Bob Seideman cheered and shook for Janis in their box, and as Janis leaned into the last note of "Ball and Chain" Stanley Mouse let out an ecstastic shriek. Even the straight occupants of the adjoining boxes were making a mechanical attempt at ecstasy, while below the entire audience seemed to sweep forward to the stage like a tidal wave, and three super groupies (Suzy Creamcheeze, Cynthia, and Claudette) got up on stage and began shaking their bodies as if it were the Day of Judgment.

Janis rooted for herself at her sold-out Royal Albert Hall London debut. She didn't jig, she jumped two feet up gleefully as the audience's fantasy expectations and projections met hers ricocheting back to them: the audience cheered, Janis cheering them. On she came, indigo bonded silk jersey shining, her voice's tessitura sinuously winding up from mating crane's growl to sweet something highs. Everyone leapt up, moved down the aisles, gladly taking pieces of her heart. Janis puts you on the line: you go forward or remain querulous. Like all stars, Janis is either good or bad, great or horrible, electrifying or preposterous. In London, she pretended English reserve never existed and broke down the boundaries.

English people don't raise their voices in anger; they heighten and sharpen the intonation. "Everyone in America is either straight or freaky," Janis explained on-stage. "The straights look straight, the freaks look like freaks, but in London everyone looks freaky so you have to get inside the head to see what's there." Not the most astute kind of psychological perception, but a gentle sociological distinction which England forces American culture heroes to make, since America is still a mythical country here. When American groups come over, they think that just by doing their whiz bam Crum comics bit, everyone is going to snap fingers sympathetically. Nothing doing.

Country Joe and the Fish played two sets at the Institute for Contemporary Arts a few weeks ago (the Joshua Light Show debuting here with them), and Joe arrived after wandering around the park and walked up to the microphone, saying: "There's a cultural problem here." He had had a great success in Scandinavia, and the English audience waited quietly for the music. Joe felt a void, but it was a fertile void. You've got to fill it in. You can't just appear, *California* flashing from your eyes, and make it in London.

Country Joe and the Fish has had terrible luck in London. Last year, the group played at the Roundhouse, and the acoustics were more like sea bubbles heard inside a submarine; you couldn't hear the porpoises from the minnows—no woofers or tweeters, just a blurping hum. This time around, you could hear Joe's beautiful new songs, and the blues about a sweet loving woman gone to seed on crystals powerfully conveyed his feelings about the cultural gap; the void was filled, the audience understood, and roared its approval. When the Fish jammed to "We want the world and we want it now," the place came apart. Everyone danced. Over forty minutes, the music kept recharging. Barry Melton smashed the guitar fingerboard as if he had discovered the principle of energy for the first time looking amazedly down at the broken ends, girls looking incredulously at Barry as if he were themselves discovering themselves.

Janis broke through this way, too. She made you enjoy yourself. This is what the Beatles did for Americans, and now, strangely, Janis has returned the impulse. She did it with "Ball and Chain," with "Maybe," and especially Nick Gravenites' "Work Me Lord." Lead guitarist Sam Andrew is getting there, and he backed Janis with luscious mellow deep-toned sighs, and Janis kissed him throughout the set on the cheeks like a little girl finding herself together in a sympathetic mirror. Her voice was controlled, sexy, joyful, and happy. She harnessed the musical changes as she rode them. "I don't want to offend propriety or anything," said Janis with a broad grin, "but if you wanna dance, this next one is for shakin' it up, and that's what it's all about, right?"

Someone brought up a bottle of champagne: It was a party and a romp. The spade sax player Snooky sang and danced and mimed a guy preparing to make it with his chick. "You don't need to worry about no brother or best friend taking your girl if you know how to *do* it," he shouted. He shimmied round and shook, and Janis joined in. "It's raining. A girl walks down the street with no umbrella and no clothes. She sees a guy. 'It's you!' She says. They come together in the rain."

The aftermath of the concert was equally explosive. Everybody dug it and found it hard to control themselves, describing Janis's body sound in print. Disc and Melody Maker were predictably ecstatic: "Soul—the feeling, the ability to put over a song as if you passionately mean every word, every last sound—is what Janis is all about, to the tips of her swinging corn-colored hair. Soul—plus, of course, a good helping of sex"—Disc. April 26. "Janis broke through the wall of British reserve, loosening the audience, shaking them up, opening them out and turning them on"—Melody Maker, April 26. But even the usually controlled critic for the conservative Daily Telegraph found himself drifting in a sea of words, as if blissfully describing an orgasm. "Here in fact was the comfortingly embodied voice of love, pain, freedom and ecstatic experience, a fire that speaks from the heart, warm rounded flesh." Janis came and London came with her.

—May 31, 1969

JANIS REUNES AT JEFFERSON HIGH

BY CHET FLIPPO

PORT ARTHUR, TEX.—The reporters were dutifully assembled there in the Goodhue Hotel's drab Petroleum Room when Janis regally swept in with her entourage, took over the room, and commandeered the bar. Here it was, the 10th reunion of Thomas Jefferson High School's class of '60 and the most distinguished/notorious alumnus, Miss J. Joplin, was there as special added attraction.

Her first TJ reunion ever and first visit to the old hometown in three years and she was outrageously dressed for the occasion: flowing blue and pink feathers in her hair, purple and white satin and velvet with gold embroidery,

sandals and painted toenails, and rings and bracelets enough for a Babylonian whore. Port Arthur had never seen the likes. Outside the Goodhue, cars full of teenies and oldsters alike slowly cruise by, hoping for a glimpse of the "big mamma of the blues-rock scene." as the area press quickly named her.

In the Petroleum Room, Janis heads for the bar for a "strong drink, as long as it's vodka." Nothing but bourbon and scotch, says the perplexed barman (this is Texas, you know, he-man bourbon/scotch country).

"God," says Janis, "somebody go out and get a bottle of vodka. This is ridiculous." A fast runner arrives with vodka, a suitably Joplinesque drink is prepared, and she surveys the room. "Am I supposed to sit at that *table?*" She regards a long, white-cloth-covered, intensely-lighted table on a platform at the other end of the room, where she is to conduct a pre-reunion press conference.

She walks to the table, swirls and eddies of newsmen at her heels, and stops to pose for a TV crew: "And now here's Janis taking a drink. And here's Janis talking to the Last Supper."

First reporter: "What have you been up to since 1960?"

"Ooooh, hangin' out. You know, just hangin' out. Havin' a good time. Tryin' to get laid, stay stoned—no, don't say that. That doesn't work in Port Arthur."

A reporter: "What do you think about Port Arthur now?"

"It seems to have loosened up a little bit since I left. There seems to be a lot of longhair and rock, which also means drug use, you know. It looks like it's doing just about what the rest of the country is doing—getting loose, getting together, getting down, having a good time."

Same reporter: "Does it surprise you to see Port Arthur that way?"

(The present writer interjects: Port Arthur strikes one as a dreary, dreary town. It is partially ringed by noxious oil refineries. The downtown area seems to consist of nothing but cheap, shoot-em-up bars and pretentious, 1930-ish hotels.)

Janis: "Yeees, quite a bit."

Same reporter: "Do you think you'll come back more often now?"

"I can't say, because I live in San Francisco and you just can't get any

looser than that [indulgent laughs from the locals]. There's really not any need to come here to get loose."

Movie critic from a conservative Houston daily: "Are there any of your classmates that you remember fondly?"

"A few. Most of them quit school and I'm gonna catch them after the show, at a nightclub. (Where she went to see Jerry Lee Lewis.)

"What'd you think of the Texas Pelican last night?"

"I *loved* it. I had a fantastic time. They make strong drinks and they have good groups. All my crazy friends came down from New York. I decided to show them how *we* did it, so I took them across the river, over to some funky nightclub, and everyone had a great time. Over in Louisiana, where we used to go when we wanted to *rock.*

"Waaayy back, when we were 15 years old and couldn't drink in Texas, we always used to go across the river. Don't you know what across the river is? Oh, you're from *Houston.* But if you're in Port Arthur, you're like 15 miles away from Louisiana and in Louisiana they don't *care.* So you go across the river. All those nightclubs with all this funky great Jimmy Reed—da-*da,* da-*da*—[she stomps her right foot as a downbeat] "down-home funky blues music and mixed drinks and smoke and making it out in the parking lot and alligators around— it's *fantastic,* man."

"Did you go to football games?"

"I don't remember. Um, I don't remember. I think not. I didn't go the high school prom and—"

"Aw, you were *asked,* weren't you?"

"No, I wasn't. I don't think they wanted to take me. [She cradles her feathered head in her hands and simulates great sobs.] And I've been suffering ever since. It's enough to make you want to sing the blues."

"Have your parents kept your old bedroom just as it was?"

"My old bedroom? Man, you oughta see what I'm sleeping on! A cot, this wide, in the den! I said, 'But, *mom!*' She said, 'We sold your bed, Janis, when you left home.' You'd think they'd have better accommodations, wouldn't you? My little brother wouldn't give up his room. My little sister wouldn't give up her room. [Little sister Laura grins.] Oh well, it's nice to be home. They've been very tolerant. When all my friends came over this morning for breakfast and drinks, they left. Of course, they had someplace to go, a wedding."

"How do you get along with your parents?" "Do they seem surprised by your success?"

"Yeah, yeah, oh yeah, man. I remember when I was young, someone, somebody, some doctor, told my mother that if I didn't quote straighten up quote I was gonna end up either in jail or in an insane asylum by the time I was 21. So when I turned 25 and my second record came out, I think my mother sent me a congratulatory telegram. They always had faith in me. They just thought I was, you know, misguided. They didn't know the world would change."

Woman reporter: "What about Bessie Smith? I notice you're kind of dressing in a funny way, feathers and things, like she used to dress."

"She was my early idol. She's the reason I started singing, really. I just . . . do you know the news about her . . . I just bought half of a gravestone for her because she didn't even have a gravestone."

"Who introduced you to her singing?"

"A guy named Grant Lyons, who used to live around here. He had some Leadbelly records and I listened to them and I liked them a lot better than what I heard on the radio. They seemed to have some sincerity to them. So then I started reading some books on blues and I kept coming across the name Bessie Smith. So I wrote away and got a bunch of her records and just really fell in love with her. For the first ten years I sang, I sang just like Bessie Smith. I copied her a lot, sang all of her songs."

The plump lady ramrod says, "Janis, may we ask that anybody that is here that is not from the press at the moment or with the reunion to please leave."

A Joplin friend: "Now, Janis, just kind of blend into the crowd and no one will notice you."

Fat chance. As the glo-worm suits and cocktail dresses and short-hairs (a few crew-cuts!) and careful coiffures pour into the room, she stands out like . . . well, like Janis Joplin at a high school reunion.

She is soon inundated by schoolmates, some of whom did not speak to her ten years ago. There are a few people whom she seems genuinely glad to see again.

Upstairs at the dinner. Janis is presented with a slick, black tire as the "long-distance" award. Quavering voices are raised in the alma mater: something about red and gold, it seems.

Back in the Taproom, the drunks have settled in for a long siege. Out on 5th Street, the freaks are waiting.

Finally, Janis emerges, alone, and looks about her and for just an instant, a second, perhaps, she looks vulnerable and little-girlish, almost lost and bewildered. But the moment passes and, slightly shaking her great mane, she turns and strides off into the Port Arthur night, very much on top of it all.

—September 17, 1970

PART SEVEN

SONGS

Layin' in bed this mornin' with my face turned to the wall
Layin' in bed this mornin' with my face turned to the wall
Trying to count these blues so I could sing 'em all

Memphis, Rampart, Beale Street set 'em free
Memphis, Rampart, Beale Street set 'em free
Graveyard, 'Bama bound, Lord Lord come from stingaree.

Lord sittin' on the Southern gonna ride all night long
Lord sittin' on the Southern gonna ride all night long
Downhearted, so cold—they was all good times.

. . . .
Lord, goin' to sleep now for Mama just got bad news
Lord, goin' to sleep now for Mama just got bad news
To try to dream away my troubles, countin' these blues.
                    —Ma Rainey, ''Counting the Blues''

CALL ON ME

WORDS AND MUSIC BY S. ANDREW

Well, ba - by, when times are bad, _____

Call on me, dar - lin' and I'll come to you. _____ When you're in

trou - ble and feel so sad, _____

Call on me, dar - lin', and I'll__ help you.__

man ____ and a wom - an ____ have each oth - er, ba - by, __

To find their way ____ in this world. ____

I need you, dar - lin', __ like the fish needs the sea, ____

158

ev - er your trou - ble, broth-er, I __ don't care. __

Ba - by, when times are bad, ___

Call on me, __ dar - lin', just call __ on me. __

DOWN ON ME

WORDS AND MUSIC BY JANIS JOPLIN

Down on me, _____ down on me, _____

Looks like ev-'ry-bod-y in this whole round world _____

is down on me. _____

2. When you see a hand that's held out t'ward you,
   Give it some love, some day it may be you.
   That's why it looks like everybody in this whole round world
   Is down on me.
   Oh, Lord! Down on me.

3. Believe in your brother, have faith in man,
   Help each other, honey, if you can.
   Because it looks like everybody in this whole round world
   Is down on me.
   Oh, Lord! Down on me.

PIECE OF MY HEART

WORDS AND MUSIC BY BERT BERNS AND JERRY RAGOVOY

and you nev-er list-en to me. Hear me when I cry___ at night.___

But each time I tell my-self that I well, I can't stand the pain, But when you

hold me in your arms___ I say it once a - gain. I said:

BALL AND CHAIN

WORDS AND MUSIC BY W. M. THORNTON

Here you're gone to-day,__ I want-ed to love you, I just want-ed to hold you, I said, for so

long.___

long.___

2. Love's got a hold on me, baby
Feels like a ball and chain
Love's just draggin' me down, baby
Feels like a ball and chain
I hope there's someone that could tell me
Why the man I love wanna leave me in so much pain.
Yeah, maybe you could help me . . .

Chorus:
And I say oh, oh, oh
Now Honey, tell me why
Tell me - - - - - - why
When I ask you
Honey, I need to know why
C'mon, tell me why
Here you're gone today
I wanted to love you and hold you
Till the day I die.

Chorus:
And I say oh, oh, oh
Now Honey,
Oh, oh, it ain't fair, it ain't fair what you do
Oh, oh, it ain't fair what you do
Here you're gone today and all I ever wanted to do
Was love you.

3. Sittin' down by my window
Lookin' out at the rain, Lord, Lord, Lord
Sittin' down by my window
Lookin' out at the rain, Lord, Lord, Lord
Somethin' came along, grabbed ahold of me
And it felt just like a ball and chain.

Chorus:
Oh, oh, this can't be in vain
Oh, oh, this can't be in vain, not in vain
I'm hopin' somebody can tell me, tell me why . . .
Why love is like a ball and chain.

TRY (JUST A LITTLE BIT HARDER)

WORDS AND MUSIC BY JERRY RAGOVOY AND CHIP TAYLOR

2. Yeah, I'm gonna try, yeah
   Just a little bit harder
   So I can give, give, give you
   Ev'ry bit of my soul.

   Yeah, I'm gonna try, yeah
   Just a little bit harder
   So I can show, show, show you
   My love with no control.

   I've waited so long for someone so fine
   I ain't gonna lose my chance (No, I ain't gonna lose it)
   Ain't gonna lose my chance to make him mine, oh, mine.

   Yeah, I'm gonna try (*to fade*)

MAYBE

WORDS AND MUSIC BY RICHARD BARRETT

178

LITTLE GIRL BLUE

WORDS BY LORENZ HART · MUSIC BY RICHARD RODGERS

feel just like ___ those rain - drops too _____ when they're fall - in down ___ all around

you.

CRY BABY

MUSIC AND LYRICS BY BERT RUSSELL AND NORMAN MEADE

A WOMAN LEFT LONELY

WORDS AND MUSIC BY SPOONER OLDHAM AND DAN PENN

for the new men now and a - gain ____ makes a touch - y sit - u -

a - tion ____ when a good face come in - to your head. ____

____ And when she gets lone ____ ly she's think-in' 'bout_ her_man,

she knows he's tak-in' her for grant - ed ____ and she does-n't_ un-der-

flames _____ try to push old __ love a - side. _____

A wom - an left lone - - ly _____ she's the vic - tim __ of her man _____

__ when he can't keep up __ his own way _____ No, _____ she's got to do the best that she

can. _____ Yeah, __ a wom - an left lone - ly, _____

oh, _____ that lone-ly girl, _____ oh! _____

ME AND BOBBY McGEE

WORDS AND MUSIC BY KRIS KRISTOFFERSON AND FRED FOSTER

TRUST ME

MUSIC AND LYRICS BY BOBBY WOMACK

Trust in me, ba-by, give me time, gim-me time, um___ ___gim-me time. ___ I heard some-bod-y say___ oh,___ the old-er the grape, sweet-er the wine, sweet-er the wine. Oh, my love is like a seed, ba-by, just needs time, now, to grow,___

JANIS

WORDS AND MUSIC BY JOE McDONALD

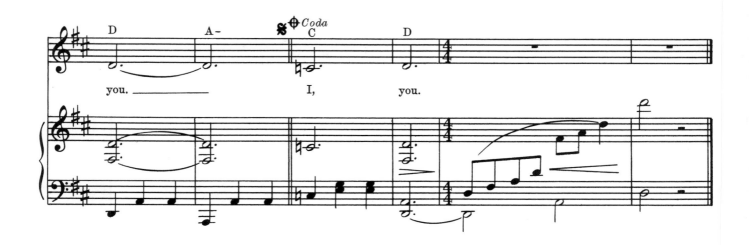

2. Into my eye comes visions of patterns
   Designs the image of her I see
   Into my mind the smell of her hair
   The sound of her voice—we once were there
   And even though I know that you and I
   could never find
   the kind of love we wanted together alone
   I find myself missing you—and I—
   You and I—you.

SUNDAY MORNIN'
COMIN' DOWN

WORDS AND MUSIC BY KRIS KRISTOFFERSON

Chorus

On the Sun-day morn-in' side-walk, wish-in', Lord, that I was stoned,

'Cause there's some-thing in a Sun-day makes a bod-y feel a-

lone. And there's noth-in' short of dy-in' half as lone-some as a

sound, _____ on the sleep-ing cit-y side-walk. Sun-day morn-in'__ com-in'

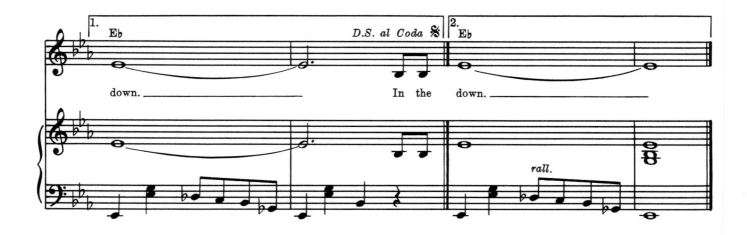

3. In the park I saw a daddy with a laughing little girl
   that he was swingin',
   And I stopped beside a Sunday school and listened
   to the song that they were singin'.
   Then I headed back for home, and somewhere far
   away a lonely bell was ringin',
   And it echoed thru the canyon like the disappearing
   dreams of yesterday.

   Chorus

TRUCKIN'

WORDS BY ROBERT HUNTER
MUSIC BY JEROME GARCIA, PHILIP LESH AND ROBERT WEIR

3. What in the world ever became of sweet Jane,
   She lost her spot, well you know she isn't the same.
   Livin' on reds, Vitamin C and cocaine,
   All a friend can say is "ain't it a shame."

   Chorus:
   Truckin'—up to Buffalo,
   Been thinkin'—you got to mellow slow.
   Takes time—you pick a place to go,
   Just keep truckin' on.

4. Sittin' and starin' out of the hotel window,
   Got a tip they're gonna kick the door in again.
   I'd like to get some sleep before I travel,
   But if you got a warrant, I guess you're gonna come in.

   Chorus:
   Busted—down on Bourbon Street,
   Set up—like a bowlin' pin.
   Knocked down—it gets to wearin' thin,
   They just won't let you be.

5. You're sick of hangin' around and you'd like to travel,
   Get tired of travelin', you want to settle down.
   I guess they can't revoke your soul for tryin',
   Get out of the door, light out and look all around.

   Special chorus:
   Sometimes the light's all shinin' on me,
   Other times I can barely see.
   Lately it occurs to me
   What a long strange trip it's been.

   Chorus:
   Truckin'—I'm goin' home,
   Whoa, whoa baby, back where I belong.
   Back home—sit down and patch my bones,
   And get back truckin' on.